"Steve's heart as a father, pastor, and teacher makes *Trans-Parenting* practical, inspiring, and informative for all parents. This is a great resource to stay focused on what matters most: building relationships with our kids as we foster their own spiritual formation. This resource should be read by every family in your youth ministry!"

— Bo Boshers
Executive Director of Student Ministries,
Willow Creek Association

"I've known Steve Keels for more than thirty years. I've watched him with his own kids, and I've seen his impact on literally thousands of other teenagers over the years. He has an uncanny capacity to understand and lead them through the dangerous shoals of our culture. Listen to him."

— Stu Weber
Senior Pastor, Good Shepherd
Community Church (Portland, Ore.)
Author, *Tender Warrior*

"In *TransParenting*, Steve Keels helps us understand the unique responsibility we have as parents to care for the leaders of the next generation. Teenagers need their parents more than ever, and this book offers solid, practical advice for influencing and mentoring kids to help them become all that God designed them to be."

— Steve Russo
International Communicator, Best-selling
Author, and Host of *Real Answers*
(a syndicated daily radio show)

TRANSPARENTING
mentoring the next generation

STEVE KEELS WITH DAN VORM   FOREWORD BY RANDY ALCORN

BROADMAN
&HOLMAN
PUBLISHERS

NASHVILLE, TENNESSEE

13-digit ISBN: 978-0-8054-3126-1
10-digit ISBN: 0-8054-3126-8

Published by Broadman & Holman Publishers,
Nashville, Tennessee

Dewey Decimal Classification: 649
Subject Heading: PARENTING \ PARENT AND CHILD
                         MENTORING

Unless noted otherwise, scriptural passages are from the Holman Christian Standard Bible, © 1999, 2000, 2002, 2003 by Holman Bible Publishers (Nashville, Tennessee); all rights reserved. Other translations quoted are NIV, the Holy Bible, New International Version, © 1973, 1978, 1984 by International Bible Society; and NLT, Holy Bible, New Living Translation, copyright © 1996 by Tyndale Charitable Trust, used by permission of Tyndale House Publishers.

Cover Illustration: Ken Orvidas, orvidas.com

06 07 08 09 10   15 14 13 12 11 10 9 8 7 6 5 4 3 2 1

Contents

Foreword

Not all authors have integrity. Why waste time reading books by those who don't? So let me begin by personally vouching for the author of this book.

Steve Keels is a follower of Jesus Christ. He disciples students. I've seen him impact literally thousands of young lives over the years, including my daughters and one of my sons-in-law. I know countless grateful parents whose children Steve has mentored.

I have never met a man with as deep a love for young people as Steve Keels. I've known Steve since he first came to Christ shortly after high school. I was his college pastor. We opened God's Word together. He was more hungry for truth than anyone I've ever known. When it came to living a Christian life of excitement and wholehearted passion, I learned from Steve, and I loved every minute I spent with him.

Later, Steve and I worked together for years on the same pastoral staff. Today he is one of my pastors. Besides Jesus and my wife Nanci, Steve is my closest friend. I thank God for him. (Even though I've dedicated two of my books to him, and I notice this one is not dedicated to me.)

Steve and his amazing wife Sue have six children, the youngest two still in high school. Three of their older children are married, and Steve and Sue are now grandparents. So as you read his words, realize he hasn't just invested his life in other people's kids, but his own. And, yes, he understands that parenting is sometimes just plain hard work.

OK, now that I've told you about the author, let me tell you about this book. *TransParenting* will help you know your children, in a way that's both helpful and fun. It will help you get more involved in your teenagers' lives and be more alert to youth culture. Understanding that culture allows you to recognize the temptations, challenges, and opportunities they face.

Too often youth pastors get the blame for students whose parents expect the church to "fix" their kids. Unfortunately, speaking as both a parent and a former youth pastor, it isn't that easy. The church can and should be a source of guidance and support for parents. But no youth group is a substitute for attentive hands-on parenting. (Not to mention on-your-knees parenting.)

I especially appreciate the wise words Steve offers concerning the critical importance of our children's friends. As I look back on our daughters' teenage years, their solid friendships with committed Christians—most of them in our church youth group—were absolutely crucial. As parents we took primary responsibility for input to their lives. Still, there is no way to overestimate the importance of their peer influences. Steve offers some great insights on making an impact on your kids' friends. This is something I've watched him do for many years. He's living proof that it works.

Steve understands the balance of truth and grace. Regarding truth, if we parents don't teach our kids to discern between good and evil, who will? The church needs to be there not only to train and guide children, but to equip parents. But no parents should wait for the church to teach their children. As Deuteronomy 6 makes clear, a child's primary education is inside the home.

Regarding grace, if parents aren't loving and forgiving, then our children won't see Jesus in us. Then our well-intentioned rules will drive them from God, not toward Him. Our kids need us to not only raise the bar high for them—and make no mistake, they do need that—but to believe the best of them, being quick to affirm and offer grace when they stumble. This will help them not to give up because they think they can't please us, and therefore can't please God.

TransParenting can help you raise the level of your understanding and involvement in your teenager's life. I pray that your young people will see in you the Jesus who came "full of grace and truth" (John 1:14). I also pray this book will equip and encourage you in the high calling of parenthood that honors Jesus Christ and leaves a lasting spiritual legacy for your children.

Parents, if you walk away from this book with one thing, let it be this: When it comes to your children's lives, no one can take your place. So, don't wait for someone else to talk to your kids about Jesus. Do it yourself. Read Scripture with them. Memorize it together. Pray with them. Go help the needy together. Give together and serve together. Show them what it means to be a disciple.

May God use this book to help and encourage you.

"We will tell the next generation the praiseworthy deeds of the LORD, his power, and the wonders he has done" (Ps. 78:4).

> — Randy Alcorn
> Author of *Heaven, The Ishbane Conspiracy,*
> and *The Grace & Truth Paradox*

Acknowledgments

This book is dedicated to my wife, who knows what it is to be a pastor's wife and to raise six kids. I love her strength and consistent affection for our family. (And, of course, to me, she's a knockout.) Sue, you're my life.

And to my friend Dan Vorm whose gifts in writing made this project possible. His theological appetite and love for his family have been a strong encouragement to me. I also thank his wife, Kerry, for her patience with Dan during this project. She is truly a woman of virtue, and I love the way she loves her three boys and her girl.

To my friend Randy Alcorn who has mentored me through the years and has had an unconditional love for my family. I truly appreciate and am honored by his friendship. Even though he has dedicated books to me (and I don't blame him because he should—hopefully, there are more dedications to me in the future), I'm sorry I didn't dedicate this book to you, Randy. This is because you made me pay for our last movie.

To my friend Stu Weber and for his many years of faithful leadership at Good Shepherd Community Church. Thanks for your friendship and your belief in the student ministry all these years.

To Gary Terashita whose quick wit and bright mind I've admired over the years. Thanks for getting this project off the ground.

To my friend David Shepherd whose vision from the beginning was to have a TQ line for Broadman & Holman. David, you're allowing us to get crucial material into the hands of students, that they might grow up in Christ.

To my friend Lawrence Kimbrough whose keen insights, corrections, and winsome spirit made this project enjoyable.

To my parents, George and Veda Keels, who to this day continue to mark my life as well as the lives of my children. Thanks for the way you love my wife and my kids. It means the world to me.

To the leadership staff at Good Shepherd Community Church. What an honor to serve with such gifted men and women who have an obvious love for their families as well as the body of Christ.

Introduction

Every parent loves to hear words of affirmation from his son or daughter.

Each year our church's student ministry holds a special dinner for all graduating seniors and their families. Our goal is to not only honor the students but also to honor their parents. A special part of our banquet is the "open microphone" segment when students are encouraged to stand up and say a few words about their mom and dad. I wish you could see the look on parents' faces as their sons and daughters speak words of affirmation and appreciation.

It's especially moving for those parents who don't yet know Christ. Those of us who know the Lord are somewhat used to hearing others share their hearts in public, but many in the world are not. For instance, I think of a student named Michael who came to Christ a few years ago from an unbelieving home. Michael's dad (a pretty rough guy) stood up and spoke about his son with incredible pride. Yet even more powerful was when Michael grabbed the microphone and began to publicly affirm his dad. It was moving to watch this strong man listen intently to his son—his shoulders went down, his head lowered a bit, and we could tell he was soaking in every word with intense concentration. It was a strong moment, and we all felt privileged to be a part of it.

Our church believes so strongly in these kinds of opportunities that we hold annual father/daughter and mother/son banquets at which children can publicly affirm their parents. Raising kids is a tough job, and moms and dads need as much encouragement and affirmation as possible. In fact, when I'm talking with a student, I often go out of my way to boast to the child about his mom or dad. I do this because I want kids to be thankful for their parents. The son of one of my close friends often spends the night at our house, and I tell the boy stories that make my friend loom large in his son's eyes. In fact, I may make the dad look a little better than he really is (he can thank me later!). The point is, kids need to see their parents as the heroes they truly are.

One of the passions of my heart is that parents learn to mentor their kids in how to love and walk with Christ. I refer to our children as the "emerging generation" because I believe it helps us understand the importance of our role as parents. These are not just our kids—these are the ones to whom we are passing the baton of our Christian faith. That's why a mentoring mind-set is crucial. We can't parent our students casually and then expect them to change the world for Christ. No, we need to make sure we ourselves are zealous for Christ, then pass that zeal down to our kids.

I have a long way to go as a dad, but my daughter Kendra recently wrote me a letter of affirmation. Here's what she said:

> Dear Dad,
>
> You are the best dad anyone could ever ask for;
> I guess I just got lucky! I love you for so many rea-

sons. I love you because you are such an example to me and others of Christ's love for His children. I love you because you are strong and I feel safe when I'm around you. I love you because you're so funny. I love you because you always ask how we're doing with the Lord even though I hate that sometimes! I love you because you are a hard worker. I love you because you listen and tell me when I'm wrong. I love you because you love Mom so much and have shown me what love and a good marriage looks like. I hope to marry someone like you someday if I'm lucky enough! You are so special to me!

Love,

Your forever little girl,

Kendra

I'm sure that after my daughter wrote this letter and gave it to me, she then moved on with her day. You can bet I didn't! I can't begin to explain how much it meant to me and how often I've read it over again. In spite of all the mistakes I've made, the fact that my girl has an honorable love for her father is nothing short of God's grace in our family.

It's this kind of affection I desire for your family as well, and I've written this book with that in mind. At the outset, I want to challenge you as a parent to:

- stay involved with your students
- stay alert to your student's culture and friends
- never, ever give up on your child
- and never stop being proud of your children.

In the following pages you'll find ideas, encouragement, and principles to help you do just that, through good times and bad. It's my sincere prayer that you'll be helped and encouraged as you mentor the next generation for Christ.

CHAPTER ONE

We Adore Our Kids!

Do you enjoy being a parent?

Your answer to this question might change depending on the day you're asked—maybe even the time of day. For instance, ask me this on a typical, stress-filled morning as my wife and I rush to get kids out of bed and ready for school, and we'll probably reply, "This is crazy."

In all my years of parenting, I've never gone to wake a kid up for school and heard him say, "Oh, thank you, Father, for taking time out of your busy schedule to wake me up at this early morning hour. You are such a wonderful, godly, and blessed dad, who always has my best in mind." Not possible. Instead, I get a range of reactions all the way from a muffled groan to a pillow over the head to, "Dad, I think I'm sick today." *Whose idea was it to have kids anyway?* I think as I walk back down the stairs. *Must have been my wife's.*

Our attitude as parents is different, though, when we catch ourselves gazing at our kids as they lay asleep at night. They look so angelic, so pure, so . . . unable to get into trouble. Right!

The Myth of Perfect Parenting

After twenty-five years of working in student ministry, raising my own kids, and meeting with hundreds of families, I've reached a conclusion: Nobody is perfect when it comes to parenting. Nobody. Everybody struggles, even the best parents. Parenting makes us face our inadequacies head-on, and sometimes it's truly humbling. In fact, I feel humbled and inadequate pretty much all the time. For instance, not one of our six kids is like another. Just when I think I've got them figured out, the Lord seems to tell me, "Here's another angle for you." My wife and I feel like saying, "Lord, are we ever going to get this right?" Yet our deep love for them keeps us trying.

Some parenting books may lead us to believe there are "five easy principles" or a simple methodology that will guarantee our kids turn out well. It's not that easy. Yes, there are things we can do to greatly increase the odds of raising godly kids—that's what this book is about. *But there's no such thing as a perfect parent.* And here's a word of advice: Don't try to become one. The pressure you'll put on yourself and your kids will drive you all crazy. Don't try to be perfect, but do strive to become mature, wise, and skillful in raising your children.

Some kids have a natural heart for the Lord and make parenting a walk in the park. Other kids seem to excel at only one thing—making life difficult. What's interesting to me is that parents may do a great job and still have kids who make mistakes. Even Solomon, who listened to his father's counsel, ended up making major mistakes in his life. That's because there are no guarantees in this adventure called parenting. Good kids can come from bad homes, and difficult kids can come from good homes. In fact, it's possible that some unbelieving parents do a better job of raising kids than do some believing parents. Usually, however, godly parenting produces godly fruit in our children. The Bible tells us in Proverbs 22:6: "Teach a youth about the way he should go; even when he is old he will not depart from it." I've seen this proven true in hundreds of families over the years. Generally, when parents have an intimate, genuine walk with the Lord, their kids will do the same.

Let's face it—being a parent is great, but it often isn't easy. It seemed simple before you had kids of your own, didn't it? You'd scowl knowingly at the parents of misbehaving toddlers and whisper to your spouse, "When we have kids, they're never going to get away with *that!*" Yep, you knew it all . . . that is, until your own little angels proved to the world that you, too, need a course in anger management.

There's something about watching brand-new parents with their firstborn child. Young parents can be extremely overprotective and are scared to death their kid's going to mess up big time. They're certain that every little act of disobedience means junior is headed for a life of crime. I used to be that way, yet things relaxed a bit by the time we had six kids. I sometimes wanted to hand our ten-year-old the keys to the car and ask, "Can't you drive yet?"

I believe parents need at least two things on a regular basis: a word of encouragement when they're doing well and wisdom to guide them when they need help. Both are crucial, and both give hope to those of us in the child-rearing years. This book is intended to provide generous portions of both encouragement and practical advice.

The Never-Ending Party

If truth be told, sometimes parents feel more like referees than parents. If the kids aren't fighting over the remote while watching TV, they're arguing over who gets to sit in the front seat of the car when we go places. That's the way kids are.

Do your kids ever play practical jokes on each other? I'll never forget the day my youngest son, Jason, took a glass of *something* to his brother and said, "Hey, Drew, I made a drink for you today." Immediately there was something wrong with this picture. Jay was concerned enough about his brother to fix him a drink? Then hand-deliver it? With a smile? Yeah, right. And you should have seen the color of that drink.

Drew took one look at the strange mixture, then, knowing his brother well, decided to apply reverse psychology. "You think I'm crazy?" he responded to Jason. "You drink it first. In fact, I bet you would never drink it yourself."

Jason, unable to resist a dare, responded, "Oh yeah? Watch this." He downed it in a few gulps, then ran to the kitchen with his tongue hanging out of his head and his eyes watering like a faucet. The Tabasco sauce he'd mixed into the cup kept him drinking water all day, trying to put out the fire flaming in his stomach. Of course, my eyes were watering, too, because of laughing so hard.

Sometimes these things are funny, but other times they plain wear us out. For instance, years ago my oldest child, Daniel, was sitting with me one day at the bank. He was seven years old and already had a tendency to blurt out embarrassing comments. I was working hard to teach him not to say everything that came to mind. Suddenly an enormous man came through the doors. I don't think I've ever seen a bigger person in all my life. I took one look at Daniel's eyes, knowing what he was wanting to say. "Daniel, God made him," I remarked as I grabbed his little arm. Daniel looked up at me with a puzzled look and said, "How?"

It's amazing how having kids can change our lives. Before you were married, all you had to do was care for yourself. Then you added a spouse, and though that took adjustment, you still had freedom to do things as a couple. You were able to do *what* you wanted, *when* you wanted. Then along came baby, and your social calendar was radically diminished. Your life was no longer your own. Of course, neither was your sleep, your wallet, or the free time you used to enjoy. It was good-bye freedom, hello diapers.

Does this mean we'd trade having our kids? Of course not. Being a parent is one of the greatest thrills life can bring. But for all the joy involved, there are times when parenting can stretch us beyond our limits. God uses our kids to show us we're not as strong, independent, and under control as we thought we were. Having children puts us toe to toe with our selfish nature.

When I think of my own kids, I can get misty-eyed in a moment. I feel like the most blessed dad in the universe. At the time of this writing, our four oldest children are between the ages of nineteen and twenty-three. Our firstborn has followed his dad into full-time youth ministry, and our second child is a business professional, married to a wonderful young woman who loves Christ. Our third works with high school kids and helps disciple a lot of girls. Our fourth child recently married a great Christian guy, and they're excited to be serving God together. We're delighted that each of our children has a passion for ministry, and all of them are actively involved in leading Bible studies.

That leaves our youngest two: Drew, our high school sophomore, works with the student ministries worship team and loves computers (what kid doesn't these days), and Jason, our youngest, is a freshman who loves sports and is involved with student ministries. I couldn't be more proud as I watch them grow in their walk with Christ. I know that you parents feel the same way about your kids. Parenting is a tremendous joy and privilege.

A Parent's Influencing Power

My goal in writing this book is to encourage and coach parents in their powerful role of influencing the next generation for Christ. Parents, we have a unique responsibility in this world. God has entrusted into our care the leaders of the next generation—the leaders of His church, the leaders of the business community, the leaders of future government. Every parent wants his or her child to grow up to make a difference, but sometimes we lose sight of the significant contribution we as parents have in the process, especially during the teenage years.

Some parents focus time and energy on their children while they're young but somehow feel that junior high and high school students need less time and attention. Granted, students might desire to give us this impression. Students desperately want to prove they're mature and capable of making adult decisions. Along with their newfound independence, teenagers usually become less communicative and sometimes more rebellious. Thus, they tend to withdraw, and parents understandably feel less needed and less loved. Parents, then, may feel less of a need to be involved in their teens' lives.

My advice? Don't buy it! Teenagers need their parents more than ever. Don't withdraw—advance! Move toward them, not away from them. This is a key component of what this book is all about—learning how to influence our students by way of wise involvement in their lives.

Parents, you are the perfect ones to influence this emerging generation for Christ, for at least three basic reasons. First, you have an indescribable love for your children. Second, you know them better than anyone else on earth. And third, they've been entrusted into your care for this very purpose.

Do you remember how nervous you were with your first-born baby? You were all about safety, weren't you? You were determined to be involved (maybe hyperinvolved) at every step of your child's life. For instance, can you remember when your first child took her first steps? You were so exuberant that you filmed six hours of videotape in order to document the event! But after several kids your reaction changed, didn't it? Instead of rushing home to grab the camcorder, you felt like screaming, *"Oh no, it can walk!"* However we're enamored with our kids' every move. Who do you watch when you go to your kid's ball games? Be honest—your eyes are glued to your child most of the time. We live and die by how well they do in sports, or by the emotions we see on their faces.

Recently, I was with my son Jason (who's my baby), driving home in the car after football practice. I found myself staring at him as he sat next to me. He was covered with dirt, sweat, and grass stains, but I didn't care. I became totally overwhelmed with the feeling of just loving my child. I felt like saying to him, "Kid, I'm just going to eat you up." Of course, I didn't say that, because teenagers don't find that cool.

Instead I said, "Jason, I'm going to tell you something you won't understand until you have children of your own. I want you to know that I love you with all my heart. I know that God loves you more than I do, but honestly, I don't know how." You feel the same way toward your kids, I'm sure. As parents, we love our children with an indescribable depth.

As a pastor, I've found that performing funerals is never easy. And without exception, the most difficult services are those for teenagers or young children. They affect me deeply. After these services, I always head home and spend extra time with my own kids; my sense of love for them is heightened. I'll lie on their beds with them that night, cuddle them, and touch their hair. I smell their scents, listen to their voices, and thank God for the joy they bring to our family. Sometimes they'll roll over and say, "Dad, you've done a funeral today, haven't you?"

Have you ever been to the funeral of a child who's the same age as your kid? You look at the parents, observe the small casket at the front, and grieve deeply for the family. You wonder what it would be like to be in their place and then thank God that you aren't. When I meet with families going through such tragedies, my heart nearly bursts. I look in the parents' eyes, and many times see no tears because they can't yet believe it's happened. Yet the depth of their anguish betrays their love for their kids. My greatest fear is to lose one of my children—and so is yours. You'd gladly give your life for the life of your child. That's the level of our love as parents.

If you have more than one child, do you remember when you heard that a second was on the way? You may have thought, *Is it possible to love this child as much as I love the first?* Of course, that question was answered the minute the second child was born; you were overwhelmed with love for him or her too. Those who don't have children can observe this kind of love, but I doubt if they can fully understand it.

The bottom line is this: No one loves your kids the way you do. Others can appreciate your children, good people will take the time to coach them, and some will even go out of their way to help them. But no one loves your children as you do. It's this radical, self-denying, all-consuming love that qualifies you to be a major influence in their lives. It reminds me of the love God the Father has for His Son, Jesus. The love we have for our students is but a picture, imperfect as it may be, of the love the Father has for His children. Yes, we adore our kids with a love placed in our hearts by God.

But there's another reason parents are uniquely qualified to actively influence their kids for Christ. Students often tell their folks, "You don't know me—you don't understand me." After hearing this enough times, parents may tend to agree. "Maybe we really don't know our kid," they'll say to each other. But that's rarely the truth. I work hard to convince parents that they do know their kids. They may not know every detail of their lives, but they know them better than anybody else on the planet.

I remind students of this all the time. I'll ask them, "Who do you think knows you the best?" Typically they'll answer, "My best friend, of course." They think this way because, as they grow, they learn to enjoy their friends at a deeper level. They share their emotions, their dreams, and their fears with each other and often spend hours talking together on the phone. Not only this, but they're going through the instability of adolescence together. No wonder our kids are convinced there's no one who understands them as well as their best friend. Yet drawing from my years of experience, I beg to differ.

Students forget that when they're with their friends they're usually on their best behavior. At home, the real teenager shows up. Imagine your daughter talking to her friends the way she talks to you. Chances are she would be friendless!

Besides, her friends never ask her to take out the garbage, mow the lawn, or clean her room. She borrows money from her friends, but "deserves" money from her parents.

Parents see their child's every mood and have to work with their student in order to see them mature. Most friends, however, won't hang around with someone who depends on them for maturity. Parents also have their child's full history in view. A best friend may know some secrets parents aren't aware of, but parents know the traits that got them to those secrets.

The third reason parents are qualified to influence their children is because the Lord has entrusted children to them that they might raise up a godly generation. My passion is to raise kids who love Christ with their entire being. I believe it's possible, and this book is about how we can influence our children at home, that they might influence the world for Christ.

A CRUCIAL CHALLENGE

So, parents, let me be up front with you at the beginning. My goal is to give you a fresh vision for impacting this emerging generation. Your role in this world is huge. Anything worth pouring your life into requires vision, and I believe every parent must have a godly vision in order to produce godly kids. I challenge you to think clearly about your parenting role and how your kids can have a part in impacting their world for Christ.

One of the many things I appreciate about the lead pastor at our church, Stu Weber, is that he's a man of vision. He speaks often of the need to prepare our younger generation for the things ahead. He desires that our church raise up a generation to whom we can someday pass the baton of ministry. We believe we're developing leaders not only for church but also for strong involvement in our community. That's exactly what you're doing as a parent. You are preparing your child for leadership in the next generation. Some parents have too small a vision for their kids. They hope their children will carry on the family name, live a happy life, and provide them with numerous and healthy grandchildren. All of this is good but falls short of the better vision we ought to have for our students. The better vision is that our kids would love Christ with an all-consuming passion and would seek to serve Him in their youth as well as in later years.

I truly believe this is why God gave us children in the first place—to raise up a godly generation that will proclaim His goodness to the world (Ps. 127:3–5). In order to do this, we need to be well equipped with basic tools. In the following chapters we'll focus on how to know our kids, understand their culture, and then develop a mentoring style that will best suit their needs. We'll also talk about the power of friends and the crucial skills involved in preventing and dealing with rebellion.

So, parents, get ready to sharpen your vision for your kids. Humbly ask the Lord for His wisdom, then roll up your sleeves, and delve into this task of parenting. Our students, and their emerging generation, will be better for it.

CHAPTER TWO

Identifying Your Child's Traits

As is true with many things in life, parenting is both a skill and an art. A wise parent will develop certain skills for his parenting toolbox, then learn to use them effectively over time. Learning to understand our kids and their unique personalities is basic to good parenting.

It's important that we learn to analyze and evaluate a child's temperament in order to parent her with wisdom. It's natural for parents to treat each of their children the same way in an effort to be fair. Certainly, we don't want to favor one child over another. But kids have different personalities. I'm amazed how kids within the same family can be so different.

God has given each of our children a basic temperament that will stay with them for life. (Some of you are saying, "Oh, great!") Don't worry—growth and maturity take place over time. Still, many of the basic traits they exhibit today will stay with them through high school, and college and into married life.

Find Their Bent

So how does a parent identify a child's basic personality? Here are several broad categories I've identified over years of working with students. I make no claim of being a psychologist or social scientist, and I'm not pretending this is a scientific study. In fact, you may disagree with how I've defined each of the following categories. I base my observations, however, on years of working with kids. It's clear that students have differing temperaments, and these categories help me define these differences. I encourage you to see them as very general in nature—in fact, your child is probably a mix of several personality types.

Also, remember that God knew what He was doing when He "knit together" your child in the womb (Ps. 139). Your child is "remarkably and wonderfully made" (v. 14a). Though some temperaments are easier to parent than others, in and of themselves they are neutral—neither inherently sinful nor inherently good. It's what the child does with her temperament that determines her course in life.

With these things in mind, we may see several personality types in our students.

The Compliant Child

The compliant child is often recognized by the following traits:

- quiet
- responsible
- able to hold strong convictions
- slow to enter rebellion

In my opinion, the compliant child is the easiest temperament to raise. As he grows up, he rarely asks, "Why?" He's not prone to question authority but instead will show submission to those over him (parents, teachers, and coaches).

A compliant child can also be very low maintenance, doesn't require a lot of worry, and is usually nonverbal. These kids are often quick to listen and slow to speak. Everybody likes this type of personality. They have very few enemies.

They can also be very orderly; in other words (believe it or not), they will actually keep their room fairly clean. They enjoy being on time for meetings, and they may not need a Palm Pilot or Day-timer to stay organized.

Compliant kids tend to be people of strong conviction—steady and firm in what they believe. As for friendships, they are prone to be singular, preferring to hang out with two or three close friends who have the same interests. They don't usually stand out in crowds; instead, they would rather blend in.

Because of their steady personality and obedient behavior, it's surprising when a compliant child becomes rebellious. Yet it does happen. I think of a young girl in our church who met a man over the Internet. This girl, though sweet and compliant to all observers, developed a hidden, online relationship. One day she decided to take off and meet the guy. Luckily, she was discovered quickly and the story ended without tragedy. Still, the parents had no idea of the rebellion growing in her heart until it surfaced unexpectedly.

Because these students don't often exhibit problems, the compliant son or daughter may receive less attention than other siblings. This is especially true if others in the home require most of the parents' time. The compliant child may actually become more obedient to make up for the difficulties caused by a rebellious sibling. Thus, it's possible for parents to lose track of the "easy child" while they focus on other issues.

It takes time to draw these kids out—they sometimes need just the right atmosphere to open up and share their thoughts.

Many parents don't realize that compliant kids tend to become quieter when they're contemplating rebellion. These kids can easily withdraw into their own secret world. Parents may think things are great, when actually rebellion is simmering under the surface.

I've found that compliant students talk within themselves much of the time. Because they can be deep thinkers, they discuss certain issues with themselves. This is normal, but parents need to draw them out and expose their inner thoughts as much as possible. When this takes place, rebellion is much less likely to grab a foothold.

If you're raising a child with this temperament, know that these students can be incredibly useful at building God's kingdom. They are steady workers and can be trusted to show up for commitments. They'll arrive on time and handle the responsibilities given to them. When they walk with Jesus, they are among the most dependable people you'll ever find.

As an example, I think of a young man whose Christian parents worked hard to stay close to him and his thoughts. They diligently engaged him in conversation and spent hours staying in touch with his world. This helped him stay strong in his moral convictions, even though surrounded by friends who chose otherwise. Though quiet and reserved by nature, he walked a path of integrity and strength during his high school years. He then went away to a Christian college, stayed pure, and is now on staff at a large church in Southern California. He is a quiet, strong leader making an impact with a significant national ministry. His parents were wise—they made it a priority to hear their son's inner thoughts and then helped shape them in return.

This temperament has some downsides as well. Of all the personalities, compliant children can be the most difficult to turn around once they've rebelled. This is because of the careful thought they put into their rebellion; they fully believe their course of action is what they really want. Rebellion to a compliant child is not done on a whim; it's carefully thought out and for that reason is difficult to correct. The chances of this happening, however, are greatly reduced as parents take time to develop, encourage, and converse with their student.

In the Bible, I see the apostle John as having this type of personality. He was the "beloved" disciple—loyal, steadfast, and dependable. He wasn't one who drew attention to himself, nor was he the life of the party. He was content to stay in the background. Yet the Gospels indicate that John was perhaps Jesus's closest friend. Jesus knew He could count on him, for as He hung on the cross, He gave instructions that John should be the one to take care of His mother. In the same way, your compliant child can have a strategic and steady influence in the lives of others. He or she may not be flashy but can faithfully accomplish great things for the kingdom of God.

THE HAPPY-GO-LUCKY CHILD

Another temperament is that of the happy-go-lucky child (HGL for short). This child:

- is very affectionate
- makes friends easily and quickly
- is talkative
- tends to live for the moment
- can be quite messy
- can be extremely open about his or her faith
- loves change, variety, and surprises

- may dabble with sin and is used to getting into trouble

One thing is common with these kids—you'll never wonder what they're thinking. They'll tell you everything that comes to mind because they love to think out loud.

They can also be extremely affectionate. They'll take initiative in giving you hugs and saying they love you (as opposed to a compliant child, who usually waits for the parent to initiate displays of affection). HGLs like to smile and are almost always looking for fun. They live for the moment and aren't too concerned about tomorrow or two weeks from tomorrow. Today . . . now . . . this moment is what counts. Unfortunately, if the "now" is not very exciting, they easily become bored (of course, they consider it their duty to let you know just how bored they are).

When it comes to special occasions such as birthdays, this personality can go nuts with excitement. Why? They love surprises—in fact, the more the better. For them change is not only good, it's a necessary ingredient for life. It's not uncommon for these kids to get excited about one thing, only to forget about it when a better option comes along. For instance, you may say, "Today is the day we're going to the zoo." This child will be thrilled until someone suggests the park. Remember, change and excitement rule the day.

For obvious reasons, these kids often have a crowd following them around. They are natural leaders, which means they're powerful kingdom servants when they walk with the Lord. When an HGL child falls in love with God and His Word, they earnestly desire to live their convictions. In fact, some of the best evangelists and Christian workers I've seen have been HGL students who are serious about their faith. These guys and gals can turn an entire campus around for

Christ. They believe everybody ought to experience a relationship with the Creator of the universe. Their bubbly and enthusiastic personalities make it difficult for them to comprehend why anyone wouldn't want what they've found. They can be very confident about their faith, even among peers.

My firstborn, Daniel, is an example of this temperament. When he got serious about walking with Christ, nothing was going to hold him back, including his love for sports. For instance, by the time Daniel was a senior in high school, he'd been wrestling for six years and had done very well. Being a typical sports dad, I couldn't wait for wrestling season to begin. Of course, I was living my dreams through my son's accomplishments (and proud of them, thank you).

Before wrestling season started, Daniel and a friend got on fire for Christ. They began sharing their faith at school, and before long they had a Bible study meeting at our house every Thursday evening. I couldn't believe how God was using these young guys. Each week eighty or more students would show up, with Daniel and his friend doing the teaching. Students were coming to Christ in droves.

Of course, I was thrilled—until wrestling season came around. Thursday nights happened to be when wrestling matches were held. I was sure Daniel would quit the Bible study and continue with wrestling, but he didn't. The Bible study was his priority; he wasn't about to let sports interfere with what God was doing.

I wish I could say I had a great attitude about the situation. But I was ticked. After all, Daniel wasn't wrestling only for himself but also for his dear, old dad. It was a selfish attitude on my part, and I'm glad he stayed with the study. God did incredible things with that group of kids. But Daniel, being an HGL with a vision for God's work, wasn't about to let anything stand in the way, not even his Dad's selfish desires concerning sports.

These kids can make a huge difference when they live for Christ. They strive to be authentic. They're risk takers for the Lord. They're not consumed with avoiding mistakes. Rather, they're usually OK with being misunderstood and are optimistic even in the face of criticism. Their inherent optimism helps them through difficult times. These students love to experience God and find excitement when His Word comes alive. They're very creative, often driven by a vision that others might not share.

As you can tell, the positive aspects of this personality are great. But there are negatives as well. These kids will wait until the last minute to make up their minds and thus go into situations unprepared. They are tempted to rely on their personalities and natural abilities instead of on the Lord's strength. They also have no problem telling their parents what they think—whether positive or negative. If they don't think you're doing a great job of parenting, they'll be happy to share how you can improve.

The greatest downside of the HGL temperament, however, is something I've seen many times. This temperament is easily enticed to sin and rebellion. If you're parenting an HGL, you know his curiosity and risk-taking bent may get him into trouble. Because he tends to live for the moment, he easily dismisses the long-term consequences of his actions. Unfortunately, these students are prone to sexual sin, because they're often driven by what they feel rather than by what they think. This is why parents need to make sure these kids learn what God's Word says about sex and relationships. Bible-based, spiritual convictions are the lifeline these kids need to hold on to.

Even then, many of these kids don't do well when it comes to holding to their spiritual convictions. The excitement of the moment can be very alluring. This personality loves adrenaline, variety, and excitement. If they don't find it in serving Christ, they'll almost certainly find it in serving their fleshly nature. It's not uncommon for kids with this temperament to come back from a church retreat completely changed and on fire for Christ, yet within a couple of weeks return to old habits.

Luckily for parents, if HGLs begin to rebel it's not difficult to notice. In fact, you'd have to be oblivious to miss it. Just as they're open about most things in life, they'll also be open when it comes to a rebellious attitude. You may not enjoy what you're hearing, but at least be thankful it's not hidden. The HGL child can be a challenge but also has the potential to change his or her world for Christ.

I believe the apostle Peter was an example of those in this category. He was loyal to a fault, such as when he cut off Malchus's ear while defending Jesus in the Garden of Gethsemane. He was also willing to go the extra mile, whatever the cost. Peter was the one who walked on water and was the only one to pledge absolute loyalty to Christ at the Last Supper. Though he often failed miserably, we can't help but admire his determination! Students with this personality may attempt bold, even crazy things for God. That's OK. You may be surprised at how God uses their gallant attempts.

So far we've examined two of the four personality types we'll deal with in this book. These descriptions are broad in scope, yet even generalizations are sometimes helpful. In the next chapter we'll continue the journey of seeking to better understand our kids.

CHAPTER THREE

Identifying Your Child's Traits 2

In the last chapter we explored the first two personalities common among students. Let's continue looking at our kids by way of these broad descriptions. In this chapter we'll discuss the artistic child and the high achiever. Again, this is not a scientific study, and I'm aware that your child is probably a mix of two or more personalities.

THE ARTISTIC CHILD

The artistic child can often exhibit the following traits:

- is introspective
- feels free to tell you everything
- notices the pains and hurts of a friend
- is extremely sensitive and very aware of the opinions of others
- creates what others think of them
- loves to spend time alone thinking and listening to music and enjoys isolation
- works hard to not be hypercritical
- struggles with cynicism

Artistic children are deep thinkers, feeling everything to the core of their being. They easily become philosophical and can probably express their feelings better than any of the other temperaments. They may love to write poetry and keep a journal or diary. They will express deep thoughts by way of the written word, through art, or perhaps with their musical abilities. These students care for others and are able to show mercy in ways other students don't think about. They have a strong sense of right and wrong and are determined in their support of the underdog. If they feel that the youth group is not caring for a certain segment of its members, this temperament will be the one that finds a remedy.

Artistic students tend toward deep conversations. They are usually quite methodical and have the ability to talk at a deep level concerning their own pains and struggles. Some of these kids enjoy open-ended questions more than they enjoy finding answers. They may find more satisfaction in the dialogue than in finding conclusions. These students articulate any anguish they feel and often presume that others feel emotions at the same level. They long for emotional depth in a student ministry, not only theological depth. It's important to them that their emotions validate their rational conclusions. Students with other temperaments can talk deeply as well, but when they converse with artistic kids, they are often in awe of the depth at which their friends can communicate.

Here's another trait of the artistic personality—extreme loyalty, even to a fault. If they feel a friend is being judged, they will remain loyal even if the friend is wrong. This happens because they focus on the relationship, not the issue at hand. Of course, in protesting the fact that their friend is judged, they easily become the most judgmental of all. For instance, if I approach an artistic student and say, "Sometimes

I feel like Joe wants to whip me in basketball," this child will have a tendency to somehow get involved. He may not know Joe personally, but every time he sees Joe, he'll look to connect the dots in building a case against him.

The artistic temperament often sees the world through more serious eyes, helping the rest of us understand issues at a deeper level. Personally, I praise God for the artistic personality. I myself can barely draw stick figures, but these students add depth, beauty, and color to many of the things we take for granted. They challenge us to back up our opinions and will actually reveal our hearts. If we have any prejudices at all, we'll find out about them through these children.

As the parent of an artistic child, you'll often be impressed by her deep sensitivity to others and to the Lord. When she's young, you'll find yourself saying things like, "My kid has such an unbelievable, early love for the Lord." This is wonderful. Her love for Jesus is far more apparent at an early age than any other temperaments. In fact, other parents may come away saying, "Wow, my kids don't love God like that."

Of course, when it comes to music, these students are often a tremendous blessing to the body of Christ. Many of them indulge themselves in the arts because these outlets feed and reveal their souls like nothing else. As worship leaders they are gifted to lead the body of Christ into wonderful experiences of praise and adoration. They help the rest of us see God in our midst and teach us to worship beyond ourselves.

These kids can be unbelievable leaders, but in a different way than some of the other temperaments. When they're walking with Christ, they can be unshakable in their moral convictions. They will stand firm against issues such as abortion, because they feel the issue so deeply. With their philosophical bent they can become strong apologists for the faith. Out of their intellectual struggles may come a solid basis for their understanding of God's Word. I think of these kids as the King Davids of our youth groups. David was artistic, felt things strongly, and was militant in his love for the Lord. Many of our more artistic students exhibit these same traits.

When I think of this personality type, I'm reminded of Anthony, a young man who led worship in our ministry several years ago. This student had a tremendous compassion for people. He had the ability to love those who were down and out as well as those who seemed to have it all together. Because of his mercy gift, he felt a passion for those who live in the inner city, and he ended up in ministry to the homeless population. Because of his sensitive and compassionate heart, Anthony decided to minister in areas where others didn't want to go. This kind of compassion is common in these students.

Artistic kids need help to not take themselves too seriously. Parents, surround them with laughter and make sure you giggle with them on a regular basis. The home must have a light and fun atmosphere, or life will become too heavy for this personality. In our household, we consider laughter a necessary ingredient of life. We enjoy sitting in the living room together as a family, laughing so hard that many of us are crying. In my mind, laughter is essential for a healthy household. If you're a serious parent by nature, rent some funny movies. Take a laugh class. Do whatever it takes to make your home bright and inviting. Your kids will love you for it.

There is a downside, however, to the deep thinking of this temperament. If these students choose the path of rebellion, it can be very scary. If you've ever seen a crowd of Goths at your local high school, you know what I'm talking about.

They're the ones dressed completely in black and obsessed with death-metal rock bands. Over the years, we've had students in our ministry get involved in Goth subculture. Most of them have this same artistic temperament. In fact, we currently have some students in our ministry who've chosen this path. They were raised in the church and appeared sensitive to spiritual things at a young age. As they've grown older, however, they've become very cynical of the church. All of them were raised in strong homes, but because they're having a tough time living for Christ, they live an almost agnostic lifestyle.

Why are certain kids attracted to the Goth lifestyle? I'm sure there are many reasons, but my theory is that most of these kids are disillusioned. They look at the pages of Scripture and try to live them out but have wrong expectations and thus become frustrated. Because of the discrepancy between what they read and how they live or because of the poor examples they may see in the church, they choose the extreme opposite. They utterly despise hypocrisy and therefore decide to give up on church and its "hypocrites." They think they've tried God and found Him wanting.

The Goth lifestyle isn't the only danger for this temperament, however. The artistic child's need for deep emotional involvement can also be a problem. One young man in our ministry was extremely passionate about Christ and very solid in his faith. He felt things very deeply and was incredible in his worship and in his compassion for others. Unfortunately, he ran into trouble during his first year of college. He took a philosophy class that challenged him about Christianity. The professor was convincing and shook this young man's spiritual foundations. Gradually, he adapted the professor's worldview, which was very tolerant toward nonbiblical thinking.

On top of this, he developed a relationship with a girl that led to fornication.

I remember talking with this student when he was home from college, and it became clear that he had changed his view of morality in order to justify his lifestyle. He wanted to get back in relationship with the Lord but couldn't part with his way of living. Tragically, the confusion in his life led to involvement in drugs, and he ended up taking his own life.

In my experience, artistic students who turn from Christ may find themselves enmeshed in a tolerant, liberal lifestyle. Some become open to homosexuality and abortion; a few end up being militant supporters of a liberal social agenda. Again, this is often the result of deep intellectual conflicts, as well as a misunderstanding of God's grace. More than any other temperament, these students need to see their parents model an authentic, grace-filled lifestyle. Even a hint of phoniness will send them running to pharisaism, legalism, or even worse. They need honest, healthy role models in their lives.

I think of King David when I think of Bible characters with this temperament. David was extremely artistic, as evidenced by the many psalms he wrote and by his great skill in playing the harp. He was also a very honest and authentic individual. He couldn't tolerate hypocrisy, which is one reason he decided to fight Goliath (i.e., "How dare we claim to serve the true God, yet allow this Philistine to mock His name!"). And finally, David was a man susceptible to his feelings. When he worshiped God, he sometimes did so with such intensity it embarrassed others (for example, his wife Michal), and his intense desire for Bathsheba overwhelmed any sense of reason or justice.

Your artistic child will need to channel her feelings and emotions into God-honoring pursuits. As she does, there may be no end to the creative ways by which she will bring God glory.

THE HIGH-ACHIEVING CHILD

The last category is that of high achievers, many of whom are perfectionists. They tend to be:

- extremely competitive
- very goal oriented
- strongly opinionated about how things should be done
- naturally gifted with many strengths
- drawn to hanging out with people older than they are
- good debaters—can be the "lawyer" of the home
- zealous for Christ, when walking with God

The high achiever tends to be the strongest personality of all the temperaments, and for this reason can mature easily into a strong church leader in adulthood. For the most part, high achievers are competitive students. They don't usually need to be reminded of their obligations, such as homework, music practice, or household chores. They merely need a nudge in the right direction.

High achievers tend to be quite stubborn and aren't concerned with what others think of them. If they decide on a course of action and everyone else goes the opposite way, no big deal—they'll just go it alone. They have the ability to look down the road and move toward a goal.

With their natural leadership abilities, these students often debate their teachers at school, if necessary. They can have very strong convictions about God and justice, and they're usually not afraid to make them known. That's why they make excellent missionaries—they're not afraid to stand alone. In fact, when we send short-term mission teams overseas, we see this temperament at the forefront right away.

They don't back down and don't care about hardship. This is because everything's a mission to them—everything's a challenge. And once motivated, they'll do all they can to meet the challenge and finish the course.

At home these students can be low maintenance because of their self-motivation. If a high-achieving student comes from a non-Christian home, he can be a powerful witness to his parents. I've seen these kids lead their parents to Christ because of their strength and consistency in the Lord.

An area of concern with high achievers is this: They can easily lead others to sin. Their leadership skills and planning ability can be used for evil as well as good. Because they're not easily cowed into submission, they won't respond to authority as quickly as the compliant child. Quite the opposite. They will challenge authority, even if only to find out how strong the authority figure really is.

Over the years I've found that this temperament will follow only strong leaders. If they don't see authority figures as deserving their respect, they'll lose interest and move on. It's not hard to spot these kids when they're not walking with God. In youth group, they'll sit in the back, arms crossed, with several friends around them. They might even lead a minirebellion or two. After all, they're not afraid to take on the world.

If you have a student with this kind of strong personality, especially a son who is a leader and go-getter, make sure you recognize his need for masculinity. If this child has a passive dad, combined with a strong mother, the clashes will come quicker and stronger—he will lead his dad and frustrate his mom. High-achiever boys will be attracted to a strong, masculine model of Christianity but will reject anything they feel is effeminate. All young men are attracted to action movies, sports, and energetic activity, but this temperament even more so. If a dad is not leading this child toward Christ with strength, he will not be attracted to the church. On the contrary, a strong dad who is not involved with church will reinforce to the child that church is for women. These kids want strength—godly, self-controlled, Holy Spirit-filled strength. They're not drawn to hyperemotionalism or passivity.

When these kids aren't excited about the Lord, they won't shut off spiritual talk, they just get too busy for anything spiritual. They don't usually become outwardly rebellious; they just find no time for God in their planning.

If you're a dad with one of these sons, get on the ground, wrestle him around, and play sports with him. This is key to building masculinity in your son. As he sees your strength and masculinity at this level, he will understand that following Christ is not just for girls. Model the strength of Christ before your sons. Let them see that real men love Christ and aren't ashamed to serve the King of the universe.

Sometimes a bad temper is bound with this temperament. Realize that these students may get frustrated with those who don't run at their same level of ability. Don't feed their tempers by being passive. Find ways to deflate angry situations, helping them become individuals with self-control.

If your child has a tendency toward perfectionism, you probably don't need to keep raising the bar when it comes to performance. Perfectionist parents can easily exasperate perfectionist kids. For instance, I know a kid who is an all-league athlete, but whose father is never satisfied with his son's performance on the field. They clash so often that the son spends time at his coach's house just to get away from Dad. I sometimes encourage parents of high achievers to back off with their expectations; most of these kids feel enough pressure as it is. They don't need parents adding more along the way.

The apostle Paul was a good example of this personality. He was very confrontational by nature. In fact, he was not at all afraid to take on the Judaizers or even Peter when he was out of line. Paul was not a peacemaker by nature, though there's no doubt God transformed his heart into that of a shepherd. Finally, he loved to learn, especially for the purpose of teaching others. He reminded Timothy to "bring . . . the scrolls, especially the parchments" (2 Tim. 4:13b). Paul was a learned man and put his education to good use in defending the gospel of Christ.

If your student has this personality, the sky's the limit when it comes to how God may use him. Encourage him to attempt great things for God, without putting undue pressure on him to succeed.

CONCLUSION

As we consider our kids' individual traits, it allows us to adjust our mentoring, discipline, and encouragement to suit the needs of each child. We can't parent every kid in exactly the same way. For instance, to say that each child will be able to drive or date at the age of sixteen is, in my estimation, not wise. Some personalities will mature faster than others. It's better to let our kids know these types of privileges are based on maturity rather than age.

I believe studying the temperaments can give us helpful insight into students' spiritual and emotional maturity. God's incredible creativity is seen by the unique way He's woven us together. Every person, and thus every temperament, is equally precious in His eyes. Study your child by studying her unique personality. You might be amazed at what a difference it can make in your parenting.

Of course, temperament and personality are only one force shaping a child in this complex world. The influence of culture is also strong, something we'll look at in the next chapter.

CHAPTER FOUR

Directions in Today's Youth Culture

Remember the sons of Issachar? Their tribe is mentioned throughout the Old Testament, yet they are referred to in 1 Chronicles 12:32a as men "who understood the times and knew what Israel should do." Not a bad description, if you ask me. God commended these men for understanding the direction their culture was going and then discerning a course of action. Parents, we must do the same when it comes to raising our kids.

There's no doubt the society in which we live generally opposes the worldview of the Bible. This leads us as Christian parents to want to shelter our kids from those things that conflict with the Scriptures. We're rightfully alarmed at what our students are exposed to on the radio, on TV, and at school. On the other hand, we want our kids to be culture changers—to reflect the salt and light of the gospel message to a lost world. There's a whole world to impact for Jesus Christ; I believe students should be challenged to engage modern-day culture rather than run from it.

Because of my involvement in student ministry over the years, I've been forced to become an observer of youth culture. Have your kids ever said, "But Mom and Dad, you just don't understand my culture"? My kids try that but it doesn't work. They're frustrated that I know as much about their culture as they do. (Sometimes I wish I didn't.) But students are the mission field to which I've been called, and having insight into their world helps me reach them with God's Word.

As parents we don't have time to be alert to every generational trend, every new rock band, and all the latest information swirling around our students. We're not able to follow our kids to school and be with them every moment of the day. We know their world is different from ours, but we're not sure how. Then again, we, too, were in high school once. It can't have changed that much, can it?

THE WINDS OF CHANGE

In a general sense, we understand quite well what our kids are up against. After all, adolescence has been around since Cain and Abel. Every generation can relate to the next if only by the fact that we share in human nature. Yet don't take for granted that your students' world is like your own. It's not. In fact, it may be more radically different than you had imagined.

Human nature doesn't change, but cultures do. For example, my grandmother remembers being taught in a one-room schoolhouse, and my grandfather was reluctant to accept streetlights because they were something new. My grandparents could never have imagined the modern-day temptations found on the Internet, or the media culture that surrounds every student.

Here are some personal observations from years of working

with students. Again, these are general conclusions and won't apply to every individual. It does represent, however, some of the ideas, attitudes, and behaviors common to today's students. The more we understand about this generation, the better equipped we'll be to influence those kids for Jesus Christ.

COMMUNICATE WELL

Students are able to talk to adults with a surprising level of ease. When I was growing up, I never addressed an adult by his first name. Previous generations understood that kids were to be seen and not heard. I had very few substantive conversations with any adult besides my parents. Now I find that students are less inhibited around adults.

For instance, think of your kids' friends when they come to your house. I'll bet it's not uncommon for them to sit and talk with you even if your student isn't home. When I was a kid, I would have come in and said, "Hello, Mr. and Mrs. Cleaver. See you later." I would rarely enter into a personal conversation with most adults. It never occurred to me to do so.

It used to be that girls were the verbal ones and guys didn't speak much at all. Now things have changed, mostly because of technology. Young men are learning to talk and converse on their cell phones, through instant messaging, and sitting in coffee shops with their friends.

In earlier generations guys would mainly talk about girls, sports, and school. Some of their best attempts at putting words together might sound like "Whaddaya wanna do now?" Now they've broadened their verbal horizons. This is why it's easier for them to converse with adults.

Some teachers have admitted to me they'd rather sit and talk with high school and college kids than people their own age. This isn't always true, but it reveals the level of conversational ability that students have these days.

Ask a student how much he spends at Starbucks each month and you'll be surprised. Most students don't go to a coffee shop to grab and go. No, they'll sit and converse for hours. Parents, think of the possibilities this gives you for influencing your student. The coffee shop might be the perfect place to casually spend some time with your child.

EXPRESSIVE WITH AFFECTIONS

In the midnineties I began to notice that students were greeting each other with a hug, not just a handshake or a "How's it going?" This included guys hugging guys. Then just a few years ago, students began to respond to each other by saying, "I love you." I hear my kids hang up the phone to a friend by saying, "Yeah, I love you too." It's perfectly normal. When I was growing up, we never said that to our friends. Maybe a man would say "I love you" to his wife and kids, but even then many of our dads had a hard time saying it publicly, as my father did. My grandfather Keels was from the generation that didn't express affection easily. A couple of months before he passed away, he said, "I love you," to me one day. I turned with a smirk and said, "What did you say? You said you loved me, didn't you?" He looked a little mischievous as he replied, "Aw, nothing."

Michael Reagan in his book *Twice Adopted* said that his dad—Ronald Reagan—was much the same way. The president, who obviously loved his son, never told him he loved him until the day Michael gave his dad a hug and said, "Dad, I love you." The elder Reagan responded awkwardly, "Um, I love you too." After that experience, the elder Reagan never let his son leave without giving him a hug. I'm thankful that my parents, even though raised in a generation that expressed love differently, always made a conscious effort to show us kids lots of affection.

When you hear your kids say "I love you" to their friends, don't read more into it than it means. It's a casual way of greeting each other. Why do students show this kind of affection so openly? Well, let me ask you a question. Do you tell your kids you love them and hug and kiss them? I'll ask kids in our ministry, "How many of you get kisses from your mom?" Almost invariably, 100 percent of the hands go up. Then I'll ask, "How many of you got kisses and hugs from your dad growing up?" Ninety percent raise their hands. We've trained this generation to be affectionate. God is affectionate with us through Christ, and we honor Him by showing kindness to one another (John 15:9).

LIVE IN A SOCIETY FULL OF WARNINGS

Children these days are raised in a safety-first environment. Fortunately, kids are encouraged to wear bike helmets and protective gear, things that weren't enforced in previous generations. Of course, much of this is because of our lawsuit-happy culture. Even McDonald's has warnings on its cups that read, "Caution—coffee is hot." Duh! Though I'm not against taking necessary precautions, I do wonder if our risk-averse culture affects our kids' mind-set and worldview. Leaders are prone to teach kids to avoid risks instead of taking risks. Somewhere, there's got to be a balance.

For example, most youth pastors will tell you that when students go on a retreat, the last thing parents will say to their kid is "Be safe" rather than "We're praying that God does a good thing in your life." How many of us watch *Dateline, 20/20,* and *Good Morning America,* then become fearful because every one of these programs capitalizes on tragedies? Parents today watch an enormous amount of news, and it's not only about political issues. Because of the media, we're confronted with tragedies all day, every day. It's only natural that we would teach our kids to avoid taking risks.

A few years ago our ministry planned an outreach trip for a group of our students. We contacted a church outside our area and agreed together that this church would host our students as we did backyard Bible clubs in its city. However, three weeks before our trip, the church administrator called us to cancel. The leaders of this church had heard about rare instances in which students abuse little children. Though we've never experienced anything like this in our ministry, the other church was fearful of the possibility and the lawsuits that might occur. We were disappointed that this kind of risk aversion kept our students from ministering to children in another area.

I can't see the apostle Paul having such an attitude of fear, can you? Paul was willing to take risks for the sake of the gospel, as evidenced by his own testimony in 2 Corinthians 6:3–10. He was beat-up, shipwrecked, misunderstood, and thrown in prison—all for the sake of sharing the Good News. Students are willing to take risks for God. Let's not hinder them by teaching them to avoid taking risks for Christ's sake.

Spend Less Time Outside

Think of your neighborhood and how many kids it contains. You may be surprised that few of them spend time playing outdoors, even on nice days. That's because this is an "electronic" generation. Kids play video games for hours. When cable TV, the Internet, CDs, and DVD players are added to the mix, it's obvious why many kids don't see any need to leave the house. Students rarely play pickup games in the neighborhood as they used to. Sports have become very specialized, and today's kids are less likely to organize games on their own.

Consequently, we have a lazy generation on our hands. If you haven't noticed, inactivity has led to obesity among many students. We have more stores on every corner, and food is now aligned with entertainment much more than it used to be. Can your kids watch a movie without eating pizza, pop, and popcorn? Probably not. When my kids have friends over, I usually run to the store and grab lots of food. It's not always wrong, but it can get out of control.

HIGHLY SEXUALIZED

Sexual things are not taboo for this generation. Many kids are authentic to a fault. For years our culture has told us to "get in touch with our feelings," and this generation has caught the message loud and clear. They're much more ready to share explicit things than we were. Their authenticity knows no boundaries.

When I go to the local mall, I understand where this openness comes from. The posters in the store windows are meant to titillate and be provocative. This kind of strong sexual advertising lures the girl who desires to lose weight, as well as the guy who wants to be seen as "sexy." Students don't necessarily have sex in mind when they buy clothes, but much of what they wear reinforces sexual attitudes.

When students talk about sex, they can be amazingly frank. I was recently approached by a senior in high school, a great kid, who walked up to me in a public setting and said, "Hey, Steve, it's been a month!" I said, "A month for what?"

"You know, a month since I masturbated." He was excited about his victory and wanted to share it with me. His tone was casual and matter of fact. I was taken aback by his openness but have come to realize that students are often this open with each other. Most parents would be shocked at the level of sexual conversation that takes place among students. This culture is training them to talk about most anything, without a hint of modesty. The young man should have approached me privately or asked for an appointment. Speaking this way in public is obviously inappropriate.

Yet it's not just boys who can be this forward. Girls, too, openly talk about their sexual attractions. Today this is considered casual talk, whereas twenty years ago it would have meant a girl was of low character. Why the change in morals? This generation is bombarded with sexual imagery from a young age. Many of TV's most popular shows, such as *Friends* and *Will and Grace,* champion the idea that fornication and sex outside marriage is fine. Even worse, many shows are meant to endear us to the homosexual agenda. It's no wonder our kids are sexualized at an early age and that they struggle to stay sexually pure. A good book to read on this subject is *The Purity Principle* by Randy Alcorn. Also, major-league baseball pitcher Andy Pettitte has written a book called *Strike Zone* that encourages students to live with purity and integrity. I highly recommend both books.

An Entertainment Culture

Kids these days have money to spend. It's at the point many parents don't know what to get their kids for Christmas—kids already have it all. And since money buys entertainment, students spend a lot of time going to movies and eating out at restaurants. Some observers have called this an adrenaline-driven generation, and I think they're right. Most students feel that if their week doesn't include large doses of entertainment, they're missing out on life.

Kids today have parties all the time. I'm not talking about drinking parties, but weekend nights when lots of students gather at a home to play video and other games. When I was young, I'd invite one friend, maybe two, to spend the night at any given time. These days it's not uncommon to invite six or eight friends to spend the night. This isn't bad, merely different. Parents love to see their kids have a good time, and I'm no exception. Around our house, the more, the merrier.

INFLUENCED HEAVILY BY MUSIC

It used to be that athletes were the greatest influence on youth culture, but I believe musicians have taken over. Much of the current fashion styles, morals, and philosophy come directly from the music our kids hear and the videos they watch on MTV. In fact, the influence of the music scene is so strong on this generation it almost can't be overstated. Technology now has the potential to impact our kids wherever they go, twenty-four hours a day.

In my opinion, students can't help but be affected by what they allow into their brains. If they listen to ungodly music, it will eventually blur their moral boundaries. Here are some examples of artists and their music styles that many students are listening to today. This is a small sample of what is selling in today's multibillion-dollar music industry. I hope your kids and mine aren't listening to them, but even so, our kids know who these musicians are.

50 Cent—*Rap.* His album *Get Rich or Die Tryin'* is typical of "gangsta" rap, which is full of references to promiscuity and drugs.

Here are some lyrics from his album *PIMP*:

Now who you know besides me who write lines
and squeeze nines, and have hoes in the hood snif-
fin' on white lines,

You don't want me to be your kids' role model
I'll teach them how to buck them 380s and load up
them hollows

Have shorty fresh off the stoop, ready to shoot

Snoop Dogg—Rap. A former Crips gang member, Snoop
Dogg is not what you'd call a model citizen. His recent film,
Snoop Dogg's Doggystyle won two Adult Video News awards
for best music sound track and top-selling tape. He served
time in prison on a drug conviction and later was charged
with murder but was found not guilty. Again, family values
aren't his strong point.

Eminem—Rap. Born Marshall Bruce Mathers III in Kansas
City, Missouri, Eminem is one of the most popular rappers to
ever hit the music scene. His lyrics go beyond crude; they are
full of violence toward women, murder, rape, sodomy, and
drug abuse. His skillful lyrics leave little to the imagination.
His most infamous song talked in detail about his specific
plans to kill his wife.

Marilyn Manson—Rock. One look at a picture of rocker
Marilyn Manson reminds parents how far the world has come
since Elvis. Manson's freakish look and satanic lyrics might be
laughable if not taken seriously by his many fans. His album
titles include *AntiChrist Superstar, Genesis of the Devil, The
Golden Age of Grotesque, and From Obscurity to Purgatory.*

Here's a sampling of his lyrics from various songs:

"The Reflecting God"
I went to god just to see, and I was looking at me
Saw heaven and hell were lies

When I'm god everybody dies
Scar/can you feel my power?

"Track 99"
God will grovel before me.
God will crawl at my feet.
These are the dying years.
These are the dying years.
When you are suffering, know that I have
betrayed you.

"Irresponsible Hate Anthem"
I wasn't born with enough middle fingers
I don't need to choose a side
I better, better, better, better not say this
Better, better, better, better not tell
I hate the hater, I'd rape the raper
I am the idiot who will not be himself

Nine Inch Nails—*Rock.* This band's lead singer, Trent
Rezner, was once a student at Wheaton College near Chicago.
It appears that he now hates everything Christianity stands
for, as seen from the song "Heresy":

He sewed his eyes shut because he is afraid to see
He tries to tell me what I put inside of me
He's got the answers to ease my curiosity
He dreamed a God up and called it Christianity
God is dead and no one cares
If there is a hell I'll see you there
He flexed his muscles to keep his flock of sheep
in line
He made a virus that would kill off all the swine

His perfect kingdom of killing, suffering and
pain
Demands devotion atrocities done in his
name . . .
And no one cares drowning in his own hypocrisy
And if there is a hell I will see you see you
there . . .
Burning with your God in humility
Will you die for this?

Christina Aguilera—Pop. I'll let her own words sum up her philosophy on life: "It's funny how society places such strict standards upon young blonde females. We're supposed to play the clean-cut view the public wants of us. But I am not your little cookie-cutter virgin."

Janet Jackson—singer. If you watched the halftime show of Super Bowl XXXVIII (February 2004), you're no stranger to Janet Jackson. With the help of fellow performer Justin Timberlake, her right breast was indecently exposed to an audience of millions on network television. The lyrics to her songs are equally explicit.

"Sexhibition"
I . . . cause I wanna sexplore you
I . . . put my hands up on you (babe)
I . . . wanna feel your sexplosion
I . . . and I'm gonna take you on a sexcapade . . .
Relax . . . it's just sex

Then there's MTV, which showcases the above artists and hundreds more. In 2001, the cable TV channel celebrated its twentieth anniversary and is largely recognized as jump-starting the music video revolution. Here are some statistics:

- Incredibly, MTV reaches more than 350 million households worldwide.
- Eighty-two percent of its viewers are twelve to thirty-four years old, with 39 percent younger than eighteen.
- And just in case you think it's not popular with today's youth, statistics show that between 70 and 80 percent of teenagers tune in for an average of around six hours each week. No wonder MTV is the most recognized network among teenagers and young adults. (See www.mediafamily.org/facts/facts_mt_print.shtml.)

Parents, if you're not sure what your students are listening to, I encourage investigation on your part. I believe I can say with authority that the above musicians (along with many others like them) should have no place in the lives of your children. Period.

EXPECT EXCELLENCE

If you watch the original *Star Wars* movies, you'll be surprised at how cheesy they appear compared with today's standards. Current video games and movies offer incredible realism so kids are bored if graphics don't look up-to-date. The church is now pressured to "perform" at a level that matches the culture. We don't need to fall into that trap, but we should be aware of it, nonetheless.

Television commercials are a great example. Advertisers will spend millions of dollars on a short, thirty-second commercial. They know it has to be produced with excellence in order to sustain consumer interest.

TAUGHT TO QUESTION AUTHORITY

Maybe you've noticed that most students don't "salute and execute" when asked to do something. They're not afraid to question authority, and their favorite phrase may be "Why should I?" Kids today often see adults as peers, rather than authority figures who need to be obeyed.

Recently, I heard of a teacher who took a defiant student to the principal's office. Along the way he placed his hand on the student's shoulder to guide him. The boy's parents are now trying to get the teacher fired because he touched their son. By placing ridiculous restrictions on teachers and authority figures, we've actually put the kids in control.

Do you remember when teachers were allowed to spank students who disobeyed in class? My teachers would use paddles with holes in them so the paddle could swing faster. (Ouch!) Today, if a teacher were to spank a student as in the 1960s and '70s, the parents would be on *Dateline* making it a national issue. Unfortunately, today's students are allowed to speak with disrespect; they get away with it because authority figures have their hands tied.

NOT NECESSARILY LOYAL TO INSTITUTIONS

This may be partly due to the ethnic blending in America, which has brought cultural diversity. I don't hear students say they're Catholic, Protestant, or Episcopalian, as did previous generations. Instead of identifying themselves as members of a certain church, they'll say "I attend" a particular church. Students are less likely to draw distinctions between denominations or even religions.

It used to be that if Dad was a millworker, the son would follow in his footsteps. If Dad joined a trade union, the son would too. Today it's not the same. Students aren't nearly as inclined to express loyalty to traditions or organizations.

USED TO BLENDED FAMILIES

Every time I ask our students how many are from divorced homes, the response is always 50 percent or above. In my growing-up years, I had very few friends from divorced homes. Now we're living in a culture of divorce. Unfortunately, this has affected the younger generation in a profound way. The lack of a stable home life has contributed to many of the problems we see in schools. Even if a child survives divorce relatively well, statistics show he is more likely to be divorced himself later in life. It can become a tragic cycle.

As a youth pastor, I wish I could say that divorce isn't damaging. But it does have a lasting affect on students. This is not meant to accuse parents who've experienced the pain of a broken marriage. I know many divorced people who do a great job of parenting. However, if we're preparing the next generation to be *in* the world and not *of* it, we need to be honest regarding the facts. Parents must do everything in their power to avoid divorce, if for no other reason than the well-being of their children.

GENDER CONFUSED

A current trend in our culture is that of blending masculine and feminine traits. Men are encouraged to become softer, more in touch with their feelings, and leave masculine traits behind. Some of this is because of the mainstreaming of the homosexual lifestyle and culture. Popular television shows like *Queer Eye for the Straight Guy* have recast masculinity in terms of the artsy, effeminate male model. Sensitivity is a good thing, but boys must learn to be men, not women. Girls, on the other hand, are coached to be aggressive and masculine in their behavior.

This is especially true in athletics. I'm not against girls in sports. My own daughter played high school soccer and had a fantastic experience. Yet she remained feminine in the process. It bothers me that coaches and dads often scream at their female athletes the same way they scream at boys. If you doubt what I'm saying, go to a club soccer game sometime. Even with younger ages, you'll often see male coaches screaming angrily at precious little girls. It's allowed because our culture pushes young women to act as tough as men.

The gender-confusion debate is rampant on our high school and college campuses. For instance, the president of Harvard University recently ignited a firestorm by suggesting that men, overall, were better at math than women. Whether or not this is true, the fact is our culture will not tolerate any perceived differences in gender. This generation is bombarded with the philosophy of gender neutrality. In other words, young men are encouraged to accept a more feminine role, while girls are pushed to become more masculine.

Moral Absolute or Cultural Suggestion?

Obviously, much more could be written regarding this culture. Perhaps, though, this will help us understand at least some of what our kids are facing. I wish we lived in a more innocent age. The truth is it's tough to live for Christ as a student in this culture. That's why I challenge parents to positively influence their students for Christ. Today's students are facing tremendous pressure to drift with the godless current of our age.

Implied in this chapter is the fact that parents must discern between moral certainties and personal preferences. Many of the directions I've discussed, such as sexual behavior and provocative dress, do in fact deal with moral absolutes. Some trends, however, are morally neutral. We get into trouble when we confuse the two.

For instance, these days high school boys wear earrings. Twenty years ago this meant a guy was either gay or part of a motorcycle gang. Today it's purely fashion. It used to be a sign of rebellion but not anymore. To the average student, it has no connotation of evil.

One day my son Daniel came home and said, "Dad, I'd really like an earring." I told him I didn't want him to wear one. Over time, however, I reconsidered. He had developed a strong walk with the Lord, his heart was right, and to him it was purely a fashion statement. Finally, I said OK—I was convinced it didn't reflect a rebellious heart or attitude.

As a pastor, however, I got feedback from some in our church who were very concerned. I got notes in my box at work, voice messages, and people stopping me in the hall in order to share their concern. I encouraged them to not interpret the earring in light of what it meant when they were young. I used the Christmas tree as an example. Many Christians aren't aware that a decorated tree was a pagan symbol during the Dark Ages. However, the meaning has changed over the centuries. Today, most Christians have no problem putting a tree in their home during the holidays. Does this mean we're all pagans? Of course not. The meaning has clearly changed over time.

We need to view some of our kids' fashions this same way. Unless the symbol or clothing is clearly suggestive, immoral, evil, or defiant against authority in some way, let's be careful we don't make a mountain out of a molehill. On the other hand, if our child uses clothing, symbols, or fashion to promote immorality or rebellion, let's do everything we can to set proper boundaries.

I remember when long hair became popular with boys in the 1960s. It represented defiance, and parents would say, "Cut your hair—it makes you look like a girl." By the time the 1970s rolled around, not only were students wearing long hair but so were their parents. It no longer had rebellious connotations; it was merely the fashion of the day. These days, students will often dye their hair different colors. Not normal colors—I'm talking blue, green, or red. In the 1980s, this identified an individual as part of the punk rock scene—very antiestablishment. These days it's much more mainstream. Though it may look silly to you and me, it probably says little regarding the heart of the student.

I'm neither endorsing nor criticizing earrings or hair colors, but I do encourage parents to focus on the heart rather than external appearance. Our tendency is to prohibit our kids from certain behaviors because we want to protect our reputations. This is certainly every family's prerogative. However, if other parents allow their kids to do something you wouldn't, don't immediately jump to the moral high ground. Even the apostle Peter had a difficult time moving from externals to internals, when God told him that all foods were now "clean" (Acts 10:9–16).

CONCLUSION

Let me end this chapter with a warning to parents. The cultural trends of today are certainly different from those of the sixties, seventies, eighties, and possibly even the nineties. Because of this, our tendency as parents is to think our generation was "squeaky clean" compared to today's. I once asked a bunch of men in their forties and fifties if they had ever heard their parents say, "Our generation was better than yours." Every single guy nodded his head yes. You see, we all remember the "good old days" and thus tend to forget that every generation deals with a different kind of crud. Those who say this current generation is worse than all others may be forgetting that Hitler and Mussolini were killing millions of people sixty years ago. And let's not forget the rallying cry for the hippie generation, Woodstock, which was full of nudity, sex, and despising authority. Then there were the racial tensions of our parents' generation, which fostered hatred and murder.

Every generation has its own junk, and our students have to deal with it as we did. Let's help them by being alert to the times and love them by not being prejudiced against them. By doing so, we can influence them powerfully for Christ.

CHAPTER FIVE

Mentoring Your Child in God's Word

Parents, what's your vision for your children?

When I think of vision, I'm reminded of the business world. Over the past decade it's become popular for businesses and organizations to develop vision statements. It helps them determine exactly where they're headed, then stay on course over the long haul. Most people in business know what they want to achieve and when they want to achieve it. Businesses will spend large amounts of time and money in order to achieve their vision. If they need to send personnel to seminars or buy new equipment for the office, they'll do it. No expense is spared in reaching the goal.

Often we parents have a clearer vision for our jobs than we do for our kids. Instead of clarifying parenting objectives and thinking through how to meet them, we play it by ear, hoping that our kids reach adulthood in one piece. There's a better way, however. Just as a CEO has the job of guiding a company in its overall vision, so parents are called to guide their homes. Successful parents will set the spiritual vision for their kids, then take active steps to help them achieve it.

A Spiritual Vision for Your Child

Mom and Dad, you are the greatest influencers on this emerging generation. Coaches, teachers, and youth pastors can be incredibly helpful, but you are the CEO of your family. Set the vision, determine the objectives, execute a plan. This goes against those who believe that as children grow older, the influence of the parents should decline. On the contrary, I strongly believe that parents should actively mentor their kids all through their high school years and even beyond. Of course, mentoring will be unique for different ages and different kids, but the vision must be there, nonetheless.

Remember, no one loves your kids as you do. Other people may like your kids, and many adults will influence them profoundly. But the primary responsibility belongs to you. Ask God to give you a vision for what He'd like to do in your children's spiritual lives.

Some friends of mine, Ralph and Myrna, have done an excellent job setting the spiritual vision for their home. Their youngest son, Jonathan, was a member of our student ministry, and he experienced all the temptations and pressures young people face. In fact, like most kids there were times he struggled with wanting to make church a priority. Yet because of his parents' faithful example, he's enjoyed a strong walk with the Lord. This couple believed they were to be the primary influencers in their son's life—all others were icing on the cake. They understood the word in 1 Timothy 3:12: "Deacons must be husbands of one wife, managing their children and their own households competently."

How did they do this? They made sure to invite Christ

into their family's daily life. Many times when they'd get into the family car to go somewhere, Myrna would say to Ralph, "Honey, would you lead us in prayer before you leave?" This made a lasting impact on Jonathan, though at times it made him uncomfortable or embarrassed. Sometimes, they'd pray so long that Jonathan would fall asleep. He'd wake up and they were still praying. He'd think to himself, "We're only going to the store." Still, this is one way Mom and Dad made Christ real, and it affected Jonathan greatly.

TAKE RESPONSIBILITY FOR SPIRITUAL GROWTH

One day a couple came to see me in my office, very concerned about their son's lack of spiritual interest. They informed me that, as the youth pastor, I was primarily responsible for his spiritual shortcomings. They felt I was not teaching what needed to be taught, and thus the youth group was not helping their child grow in the Lord.

Whenever I hear things like this, I sympathize with the parents' point of view. I realize I'm dealing with parents' most treasured possessions—their children. Parents feel strongly about every facet of their child's lives, including the church youth group. I understand this and am open to positive criticism. In fact, I want to work closely with parents and support them in the tough job of rearing this generation.

On the other hand, I cannot take primary responsibility for every student's walk with Christ. That responsibility lies with the parents. The Bible encourages adults to take charge of the household, leading kids into a genuine walk with God. As a youth pastor, my job is to assist them in that task.

A clear teaching concerning parental responsibility is found in the book of Deuteronomy, chapter 6. Look carefully at the command found in this passage: "These words that I am giving you today are to be in your heart. Repeat them to your children. Talk about them when you sit in your house and when you walk along the road, when you lie down and when you get up. Bind them as a sign on your hand and let them be a symbol on your forehead. Write them on the doorposts of your house and on your gates" (vv. 6–9).

This doesn't sound like passive parenting, does it? When God tells us to repeat these commands to our children, He's making it clear that parents have a huge task placed squarely on their shoulders. It's an enjoyable task and extremely satisfying—but huge, nonetheless.

A Practical Word to Dad

Dad, let me talk to you for a moment. One thing I've noticed over the years is this: If Dad is not a spiritual leader, some kids will refuse to let Mom take that role. I don't say this to denigrate or lessen the mom's influence in the home. Not in the least. But some kids, especially strong-willed sons, need the strength of a dad in order to reach their spiritual potential. Fathers must take spiritual initiative, especially with their boys.

I've seen fathers who do a great job mentoring their boys in sports. One father I know was extremely bright theologically but rarely talked to his son about spiritual matters. This man spent hours teaching his boy how to catch, throw, and hit a baseball. Unfortunately, he spent more time on the mechanics of the game than on the character qualities that make a good athlete. When his son would pout like a baby and not play well with others, the dad was extremely tolerant. Maybe it was because these same attitudes were tolerated in him as he grew up. Whatever the reason, it seemed clear the dad's vision for his son revolved primarily around athletics. Unfortunately, he handed over the spiritual mentoring to me, the youth pastor.

Even men who understand Scripture may find it easier to talk with their kids about hobbies than about spiritual matters. I think all men have this tendency, and I do as well. I love athletics and often wake up in the morning with sports on my mind. I can't wait to watch my kids at their games and sporting events. But, Dad, mentoring is more than teaching kids how to catch a ball or make a good tackle. Sports are great, but it's crucial that we train and instruct our kids to love Christ. We've got to be proactive in this area. In Ephesians 6 fathers are called to train and give instruction "in the Lord" (v. 4). It doesn't get any clearer than that.

Let's define it further. Good character is important, but effective mentoring is more than just imparting morals. I know unbelievers who are great at teaching their kids right from wrong. In fact, some non-Christian families do a better job of teaching morals than some within the church. To be honest, good kids are a dime a dozen, and they don't all belong to Christian families. Our goal must be more than raising good, moral kids; we must aspire to raise students who are diligent in their love for Christ. There's a big difference between the two.

Is this the vision you have for your child? Examine your heart by asking yourself this question: "Which of my child's achievements excite me most?" Grades, sports, or scholarships? Financial success or perhaps marrying just the right person? These things are nice, but we should be most excited when we see solid, spiritual growth in our children. We need to dream about our sons and daughters marrying godly mates, then raising their kids in the church. We should dream about our young men becoming elders in the church's next generation, and our daughters serving Christ together with their husbands. Here are the types of dreams all parents should have for their kids:

- standing firm in their faith
- becoming missionaries
- starting a business and giving 50 percent to the church or to missions
- starting and leading Bible studies with their friends
- having a good understanding of apologetics and using their knowledge to defend the faith
- being willing to die for the faith

These things should bring true excitement to our hearts. Why? Because these are the desires of God's heart. They carry with them eternal reward and a fulfillment that comes only from investing in the kingdom of God.

AN ATTRACTIVE WALK WITH GOD

Looking again at Titus 1, we're told two times that leaders need to be blameless (vv. 6–7). Notice it doesn't say flawless. Our kids don't expect us to be perfect, but they do desire to see the attractiveness of Christ in our lives. This generation will allow us as parents to be their mentors; we just have to believe it.

Our kids will model what they see in our lives. One time I made a mistake with one of my boys, punishing him for something that wasn't his fault. Our family had driven separately to a school play, and after it ended I asked Daniel to gather his brothers and meet me at the car. I was very impatient, wanting to beat the crowd out of the parking lot. I waited . . . and waited . . . and waited . . . but still no family! By this time I couldn't see straight because of my frustration. I finally went in, found Daniel, then shared with him all the way home why he was in big trouble.

Still fuming mad, I sent Daniel to bed early (even though it was a Friday night). For a long time I could hear him upstairs doing the hiccup cry, saying, "But, Dad, I want to tell you something." After I'd finally settled down enough to listen, I sat on his bed and heard his side of the story. He reminded me that he'd come with Mom and didn't know where my car was parked. Boy, did I feel like an idiot—I'd really blown it.

I got him out of bed, gave him a hug, and as part of my apology, took him to the store for ice cream. As we walked from the car to the store entrance, I felt his little hand reach up and grab mine. He saw that I felt horrible, and he willingly forgave me for what I'd done. Just as I love him unconditionally, he was showing me his own unconditional love. Don't think that because you're not a perfect parent you don't have the right to mentor your child. Approached correctly, your child will give you permission to build spiritually in his life.

Sometimes we're discouraged from spiritually mentoring our kids because we have wrong expectations. We look at people like Billy Graham and James Dobson, and when we hear them speak, we naturally put them on a pedestal. We think to ourselves, *Now there's a guy who can mentor his kids. But how could I ever do that?* Our flaws loom large in front of us; we feel we're too ordinary for the task. I'm sure, however, if you asked Mrs. Graham and Mrs. Dobson if their husbands are perfect, they'd set you straight. Or better yet, ask their kids. Every one of us is human and makes mistakes. Unfortunately, we idolize others, and this tends to defeat us. We tend to believe we can't live an attractive example for our kids because they know us too well.

Mom and Dad, work hard at being authentic in your walk with Christ. Besides praying for your children, it's probably the single most important thing you can do. It doesn't matter if you have glaring imperfections. Maybe you're deep in counseling, working through issues, and wondering how you of all people can raise your kids well. More than perfection, your kids want to see in you a deep love for Christ. They want to know that you're on the journey, not that you've arrived. When children see that our identity in Jesus is more important than the job we do (doctor, lawyer, policeman), they will find themselves attracted to the God we serve.

TRAIN YOUR CHILD TO DISCERN

The Old Testament prophet Isaiah said, "Woe to those who call evil good and good evil" (Isa. 5:20a). As mentors to this emerging generation, we are responsible to teach good doctrine to our children and help them discern between truth and error. I've talked with many students over the years who've been enticed to join various cults or even aspects of the occult. It happens because they have little doctrinal discernment. Surprisingly, some of these kids are from strong Christian homes. The wise parent will not leave all teaching to the church but will talk with kids about correct doctrine. When done in a casual manner, not as a lecture, students will usually respond positively.

One young girl in our ministry was as bubbly and sweet as they come. Though her parents were strong believers, they weren't concerned when she started dating a nice young boy who was Mormon. They'd never studied Mormon doctrine and were impressed by the boy's good morals and clean-cut appearance. Over time, the daughter fell in love with the young man and joined the Mormon Church in order to get married. Of course, now the parents have learned the doctrinal differences between Mormonism and Christianity and understand the error in Mormon teaching. They wish they had taken the time to study when their daughter began the relationship.

There have been times my kids have become tired of my talking to them about Christ. I don't really care—I do it anyway. I don't wait for them to come to me with spiritual questions, though I love it when they do. Instead, I approach them with questions, ones that are hard to answer and cause them to think about spiritual issues. I appreciate it when people do the same with me. For instance, there may be times when I don't want my wife to speak truth into my life. She does it anyway, and I'm glad she does. Sometimes my closest friends will ask me tough questions, holding me accountable in my walk with God. Again, it's not always comfortable, but I'm glad they take the risk. In the same way, I need to hold my kids accountable in their spiritual walk. This is one way I can help them discern between good and evil.

BECOME A SELF-FEEDER

In order to influence our students for Christ, we first must have something to say. Parents can talk about the traditions of their home and what life was like when they were young. But only parents who are full of fresh truth from God's Word can speak this truth into the life of their child.

To be a self-feeder means having our own daily devotional life. If I as a parent read only a verse a day and call it good, I'll have very little to pour into my child. When I then attempt to speak to my son or daughter about spiritual things, my talk will remain on the surface. If you've ever tried to fake spiritual maturity, you know what I'm talking about. It just doesn't work. Our minds and hearts must be full of God's Word and its application to daily life.

Let me encourage you to make a fresh commitment to Bible study and prayer. As a parent, your walk with Christ affects not only you but also the lives of those under your care. It's true that the spiritual life is "more caught than taught." Let's be sure what they catch from us is a life devoted to Christ.

One of the greatest sins we can commit as parents is to teach our kids that God is boring. Of course, we'd never say He's boring, and we may not even think it to ourselves. But by the way some parents act, they might as well be shouting it from the rooftop. I need to ask myself searching questions once in awhile: How often do I get excited about what God is doing in my life and the lives of others? Do I rejoice at God's activity? Do my kids ever see me studying the Bible? Is my prayer life contained to saying a blessing at the dinner table? Do I get more excited about sports, TV, movies, or my job than I do about seeing God at work? We need to ask ourselves these questions on a regular basis.

The challenge is especially real for parents raised in church. As wonderful as this is, sometimes the longer one sits in the pew the more sour he becomes. It's possible to develop a know-it-all attitude that says, "I dare you to teach me something I haven't already heard." Without wanting to, many of us have made Bible study something boring and dreary. We've gone to church for years, so it's routine. Somehow, we're satisfied with what we know about God. Maybe the trials and distractions of life have left us bitter and cynical. Whatever the reason, if we've left our first love (Rev. 2:4), we need to discover Him once again. This is crucial for any parent who desires to influence a son or daughter for Christ.

THE ART OF ASKING QUESTIONS

One of the best ways to mentor our students in the Bible is by asking good questions. Students love to be challenged, and this is a great platform for Bible study and exploration. By asking difficult questions concerning God and His Word, we create an environment of learning and curiosity. It teaches them that learning about God is worthy of diligent effort.

One morning I was asked to speak to a group of Christian athletes at the local high school. I know this is a generation that likes to be challenged, so I began by asking several questions. I said, "We all know that Jesus came to be the Savior of the world. Is that right?" Everyone agreed. Then I asked, "If God wants men to be saved, why didn't He just save everybody at the start? Why didn't He say, 'Look you're all saved'?"

I could see them scratching their heads and could tell I had them thinking. I continued, "Why did God have to become a man? How *can* God become a man? Did His deity cease? But if that's true, how can God cease to be God?"

By this time the kids' brains were really churning. I could almost see smoke coming out their ears. Then one kid said, "Well, maybe His deity stopped."

"OK," I continued, "so God can cease to exist, is that right?" I then shared with them that there are some things God cannot do—He cannot cease to exist and He cannot lie. From there the conversation started rolling, and we opened our Bibles and started our study.

This has become my favorite way of teaching the Bible. I ask questions of my kids at home, and I ask questions when leading Bible studies for students in my office. Students love to think, and this is a great way to keep them engaged. Here are the types of questions I love to ask:

- Who created God?
- Has He ever been lonely?
- If He's not lonely, why did He create mankind?
- Where did He get the matter by which to create?
- If God is eternal, is there space on the other side of God?
- Did God create space, or has it always existed?
- If Jesus was born of Mary, then was He half human and half God?

These aren't simple questions, are they? They can't be answered with a simple yes or no. That's why they lead to unbelievable discussions. Students want the answers right away, but sometimes I don't give them until the next day. My goal is not to make it easy but rather to complicate things a bit. I want to create in students a thirst for the Word.

Some of us have made Bible study anything but exciting— we're bored and our kids know we're bored. Sometimes those who've walked with God for years have stopped asking difficult questions. This prevents the mind from learning. What a shame. Our kids need to see us hungry for God's Word. If we're not, why should they be different? This emerging generation wants to be challenged concerning spiritual truth. Parents, don't just ask about their day, their friends, and how many points they scored in a basketball game. Learn to ask theological questions, then be prepared to give an answer.

At this point, some of you are saying, "Yeah, right. I don't know anything about theology. I can't even ask the questions, let alone begin to answer them!" OK, then start simple. Instead of many questions, ask only one question. Then do some study and find the answer. The goal is to create a tension in your student that drives him to learn more about God through His Word. Don't expect big long discussions. Just throw a question out there, talk awhile, and then come back to it another time. In this way students become defenders of the Bible, not just observers.

CREATE SPONTANEOUS MOMENTS

In my experience, some of the best opportunities for mentoring are found in spontaneous moments. Just as we saw in Deuteronomy 6, it's during normal activities of daily life that opportunities for mentoring abound. For instance, when I get into the car to drive my kids somewhere (which is constant, believe me), I talk with them about the most recent thing God is doing in my life. This works especially well when I'm with them one on one. I'm not looking for a doctrinal dissertation in response. Rather, I'm looking to raise real-life issues from God's Word in a real-time environment.

When I have these conversations, I usually don't expect much in the way of reply. That's just the way kids are. When you ask a junior high boy how he's doing with the Lord, he'll say, "Good." Sometimes that's all I get. It's the same when I ask him about school: "Fine" is usually the extent of it. (Of course, ask a junior high girl the same questions, and you might as well extend your trip, especially if she's in the mood to talk.) No, I don't expect a deep discussion each time I'm in the car with my kids. But I do want them to constantly hear about their dad's walk with Christ. If nothing else, they'll know that their dad is excited about the Lord.

Another way to create spontaneous moments is to go into your kid's room at night. Sometimes if you just sit there, you'll be amazed at what comes out of his mouth. Don't correct, don't freak out, and don't overwhelm. A mentoring parent will hear things he or she wouldn't hear otherwise, and the parent stays in process with the child's spiritual growth.

Another idea, not quite so spontaneous, is to take your child to Starbucks. Take your Bible and read a passage together, or share what God has taught you within the past week. It might be only five minutes of spiritual talk, but that's OK. I'll take these five minutes of pure gold anytime!

A word of warning, however: Never use times like these to confront your child about everything she does wrong. Don't use the Bible to berate her for not cleaning her room. Rather, go after her heart. If you're too quick to lay down rules and regulations without first going for the heart, any obedience on her part will probably be short lived. Focus on God's grace and forgiveness. A coffee shop is a great place to enjoy God's Word together in a nonthreatening environment.

Many families aspire to have family devotions, but I have to admit formal devotional times have never worked well for us. If they work for you, that's great. For our family, they seem unnatural. We tried to have devotions for years, only to abandon them for more spontaneous times together, as well as one-on-one time with our kids.

Why didn't devotions work for us? To be honest, our family Bible studies seemed to quickly degenerate into a fight. We'd be sitting in a circle with a three-year-old and an eight-year-old, and I would say, "Be quiet. We're going to love Jesus now."

One of my kids would say, "But, Dad—"

I'd respond, "I said be quiet! We're now going to learn together about Christ and His love!"

As I said, families are different. Maybe your family can sit down together without experiencing World War III. For us, that format has never worked. We find that spontaneity works best in relating truth to our kids.

GO ON MISSION TRIPS TOGETHER

Another great way to become effective in mentoring this emerging generation is through short-term missions. Don't just send your kids overseas—go with them! It will provide a lifetime of memories, all centered on the Lord and the work of building His kingdom. A friend of mine, John, recently took his wife and two boys to Germany in order to reach high school students. The joy on their faces when they returned was incredible. This family will never be the same. Their relationships are marked forever by the great experience they now have in common.

GO AFTER YOUR CHILD'S HEART

I've observed parents who try to shame their kids into submission by saying things like, "You call yourself a Christian?" or "You act this way, and you're a leader in the youth group at church?" Please, parents, don't ever do this to your student, especially if he or she is growing in Christ and is serious about a walk with God. Not only is this demeaning, it can also discourage a walk with Christ. Parents who use this approach are focusing on the external behaviors rather than the heart.

We should never underestimate the fact that "'man sees what is visible, but the LORD sees the heart'" (1 Sam. 16:7b). It's not that outward appearance isn't important, but God is much more concerned about a person's heart. I often think of David, the shepherd boy, as he was anointed king of Israel in front of his dad and his brothers (see 1 Sam. 16). David's father, Jesse, was surprised when the prophet Samuel didn't place the anointing oil on the head of Eliab, Jesse's oldest son. In fact, everyone was surprised, including Samuel. But God wasn't impressed by Eliab's stature or by his good-looking and commanding presence. Nor was God interested in the other five brothers who came after Eliab. No, God was looking for a heart that was "after his own heart" (1 Sam. 13:14a NLT). So here came David straight from the field, smelling like sheep. He was the small one who wasn't even invited to the party, yet Samuel said, "Anoint him, for he is the one" (1 Sam. 16:12b).

I can imagine Jesse must have been a typical parent, just like me. No doubt he was proud of his boys, especially Eliab. I could be wrong, but I'll bet Eliab was most like his dad. I can imagine Jesse's friends sitting at the gate and saying (with a thick Jewish accent), "Jesse, that boy of yours, Eliab, he's amazing. Why, he's so tall and strong and handsome—the boy is outstanding." Even Samuel, when he first saw Eliab, said to himself, "Here he is. This has to be the next king of Israel."

It's interesting, isn't it, that God Himself would not allow man's discernment to overrule His choice. Eliab may have been the "obvious" selection in man's eyes, but David had the heart God esteemed. Physical leadership, good looks, and natural charisma will always gain man's attention. God, however, is more concerned with the heart. Let's be careful we don't raise our kids to esteem the lesser rather than the greater. Parents with a legalistic bent need to realize that outward conformity cannot sustain an authentic walk with Christ.

Several years ago I met a family very concerned with appearances. As the years went by, I watched every one of the kids rebel against their mom and dad. Why? The parents were overly concerned about their image, and they put extreme pressure on the kids to dress and act in a certain way. The kids felt it was just a show, and they ended up running away and getting involved in immoral relationships. Of course, this greatly embarrassed the parents, who would then place more pressure on the kids to "perform" their Christian duty. Every one of the kids told me the same thing over the years: "Mom and Dad only care about the family image. They don't really care about our hearts." Knowing students, I'm sure they were exaggerating to some degree. Somehow, though, this is what the parents were communicating, and the kids heard it loud and clear.

To me, this is pharisaical parenting, not mentoring. A pharisee is overly concerned about externals—what others will think. This kind of parent says, "Whatever you do, don't make our family look unspiritual." He is overly concerned with rituals, traditions, and most of all, image.

Parents, avoid raising your students to believe that externals are more important than their hearts. I remember sitting down with one of my friends while on a retreat, telling him some things his daughter had shared with me. His young daughter was the kind every parent would love to claim. She was sincere in her walk with Christ and was consistently spending time in God's Word. Yet without meaning to, her dad made her feel she could never live up to his spiritual expectations. It was killing her inside; she felt her every action was being examined under a microscope. Though he meant well, his scrutiny was stunting her spiritual growth and causing harm to what had always been a precious relationship.

To my friend's credit, he got the message. When he understood the depth of her feelings, it was as if an arrow pierced his heart. He responded by determining to learn more of God's grace and how to reflect that grace toward his daughter. He worked hard to become less critical, rather than resorting to constant scrutiny. Today my friend often refers to that conversation as a turning point in his spiritual life; he has truly learned to live under the grace of God.

It's interesting that our view of law, grace, and forgiveness greatly affects how we raise our kids. If a parent has a habit of seeking forgiveness from God on a regular, even daily basis, he's much more likely to raise his kids in a grace-and-truth environment. When I think of legalism, I'm again reminded of the Pharisees during Jesus's time. On one occasion a woman interrupted Him while dining at the home of a religious leader. With a heart full of devotion, she began to wash Jesus's feet with her tears and dry them off with her hair (Luke 7:36–50). The Pharisees were sickened by this act of adoration, but Jesus said, "Her many sins have been forgiven; that's why she loved much. But the one who is forgiven little, loves little" (v. 47). Legalists have a hard time receiving God's forgiveness because of their own pride. Legalistic hearts have difficulty showing patience to others who don't keep the "law" as they do.

So how does this apply to raising kids? Practically speaking, it means that you will seek to help your child come to know God, not just God's rules for conduct. A wise parent will help her student gain a clear glimpse of God in the Scriptures, not just a standard for moral conduct. Someday your children will be out of the house and on their own. What will keep them from making a mess of their lives? Good morals will help, of course, but a strong relationship with the living God is even better. Morality is important, but morals often change with the prevailing winds, if not derived from knowing and loving Christ. We must seek to develop Christ followers, not just good moral kids.

Your child's goal should be to fix his eyes on Jesus (Heb. 12:22), and your mentoring goal should be to help him do that, rather than fixing on his performance. For example, when you sit down for some mentoring time with one of your kids, I encourage you to not turn it into a lecture on cleaning his room or mowing the lawn. Instead, focus on Christ and loving Him. If we fill our mentoring times with lectures, kids will lose interest immediately. Draw them to God's Word and let the Holy Spirit do His work.

When I think of good mentoring, I remember a dad who approached me after a men's meeting at church. I could tell he had something to share, and before long he laid out his amazing story. His son TJ was a good kid, and this dad was working hard at mentoring his son. He spent time in the Bible with his boy and talked with him about the Lord constantly. Recently, however, a bully had been picking on TJ at school, and it was driving this dad nuts.

For some reason the bully hated TJ's guts. Every day he would find TJ in the hall between classes and slam him into the lockers. Of course, TJ did his best to avoid this guy, but the bully was making TJ's life miserable. At first the dad planned to go directly to the principal, but TJ pleaded for him not to. Then he felt the Lord prompting him to pray consistently for this bully, that God would work in his life. So this man sat down and prayed with his son every day before school, asking God to make good things happen out of bad.

TJ had a habit of reading the Bible at his desk each morning before class. Even though the bully was in that first-period class, TJ continued to open his Bible and read a few verses quietly before the bell would ring. Sometimes, out of the corner of his eye, TJ could see the bully watching him as he read.

Time went by and things weren't changing. TJ was still getting pushed around, trying to survive day by day. Then it happened! One day as TJ opened his Bible to begin the day, he looked up and saw his enemy quickly approaching. *Nuts, here we go again—I'm gonna get smacked or made fun of,* TJ thought. Yet the bully surprised him by saying, "Every morning I see you open your Bible in class, so I thought I'd tell you something. Last night I went with a friend to his church group, and I prayed to accept Jesus into my heart. I just thought you'd want to know." From that time on, the bullying stopped.

You can imagine the joy at TJ's house that evening as the family rejoiced in answered prayer. This dad could have gotten tough, taken things into his own hands, gone to the principal or the bully's dad, and probably made things worse. Of course, there are times when we parents need to step in and do our part. But in this case, think of how the dad influenced his son by seeking God first. You can bet TJ will never forget his dad's godly influence during that difficult time of life.

Parents, mentor your kids. Not through the lens of legalism nor by being uninvolved (which is liberalism). Rather, influence them to become Christ followers, desiring to walk in obedience because they first love Him. Remember, God is looking at the heart. Give correction to the externals when needed, but focus primarily on the heart.

CHAPTER SIX

The Powerful Influence of Friends

"Bad company corrupts good morals."
—1 Corinthians 15:33b

Several years ago one of my sons brought home a couple of kids I'd never seen before. "Hey, Dad," he said as I walked into the house, "I want you to meet my friends."

"Hi, Mr. Keels," they both piped in. I could tell my son really wanted to be accepted by these new buddies, and he was working hard to help me like them. Have your kids ever done that?

"Dad, these guys go to church, and, Dad, they don't cuss, at least very much," he added, as both boys nodded their heads in agreement. With a cheesy smile I thought to myself, *OK, let's get to know these boys.* I could have sat them down and asked them twenty-five questions, but instead I said, "Hey, guys, let's play some basketball." I was glad for my son; we were new in the neighborhood, and he was desperate for companionship.

His new friends, however, quickly turned out to be less than ideal. After shooting hoops, my son and his new buddies headed into the neighborhood to hang out. A couple of hours later, when my son was late getting home, Sue and I decided to go find him.

"I'll bet he's at the top of the neighborhood," I told Sue as we began our search. Our son knew this was beyond the boundaries we'd set. Sure enough, as we rounded a corner, we caught a glimpse of him on his bike, riding on the street where he wasn't supposed to be. Being a godly man, I immediately began making plans to disinherit him!

His new buddies had convinced him to go beyond our limits even though he knew it was wrong. He caved in to their influence. Sue and I kept walking, and eventually followed him a couple of miles to a large store. Our timing was perfect. We arrived at the entrance just as our son came charging out to get on his bike. The look on his face was priceless, and he froze in his tracks. I walked up and quietly told him to follow me home. He wanted to ride on ahead, but I said, "No, son, you stay with me as I walk, and I'm going to impart some wisdom to your tiny mind!"

We talked about a number of things on that slow walk home. The main topic, though, was friends. We talked about how his need to be accepted by others had caused him to quickly disregard the heart of his parents. "We love you, son. We are 100 percent crazy about you. Trust is very important to us, and your actions have shown us that you're too easily influenced by others."

Then came the inevitable question. "So how long am I grounded?" he asked. "Well, let's start with the rest of your life," I replied. Then I reconsidered—I'm not sure that would be fair to me!

Every child needs friends; good friends are a gift from God. As parents, we need wisdom and skill in learning to direct a child toward positive friendships. Let's face it, our homes and churches are in a cultural battle, and our kids are the prize! After twenty-five years of working with student ministry, I can honestly say that friendships can make or break your child's spiritual life. I've seen good kids make horrible choices because of poor friends. On the other hand, I've seen students who were weak in their faith grow strong because of choosing friends wisely. I believe there are many things we parents can do—and must do—to guide our children in this crucial area.

HELPING YOUR CHILD CHOOSE GOOD FRIENDS

Parents, do you remember when you were in junior high and high school? It seems like a different world back then, doesn't it? Yet in many ways, things haven't changed all that much. Think back for a moment and remember some of the activities you enjoyed—football games, proms, band trips, cheerleading, and parties. If you remember some of these events, perhaps you can also remember the emotions you experienced during those turbulent times. Maybe you felt on top of the world, enjoying lots of friends and being with the "in" crowd. Others may have experienced feelings of inadequacy and fear of rejection. All of these emotions, and more, are common for our kids, just as they were for you and me at that age.

What gave you stability and strength during the growing-up years? If you're like me, it was your friends—the people you hung out with for weekend activities. And perhaps more than at any other time in life, friends became a huge part of your identity. You may have felt like a somebody or a nobody depending on the people you hung around with. Students feel the same today. At school, at church, and in whatever activities they're involved, we need to remember the influencing power of our children's friends.

Just as "iron sharpens iron" (Prov. 27:17), so does ungodly iron sharpen ungodly iron. If a child has a propensity for independence, he will usually seek out those who have a like mind-set. Some kids just seem to have a nose for trouble; even at church camp, they delight in finding a rule to break or a person to pick on. Adding three or four like-minded friends to the mix pours fuel on the fire. Over the years I've noticed that such students tend to connive; it's their recreation. When they're together in groups of two or more, they rarely stop each other from making ungodly decisions. It becomes a "dare" relationship, rather than a relationship built on restraint and self-control.

Isn't it amazing how kids want to be "their own person" yet end up talking the same, walking the same, and basically developing their own little culture together? As I've already mentioned, I'm not too concerned with outward appearance, such as baggy clothes, earrings, and the like. (Someday they'll probably look back and wince at what they're now wearing, as we do when we revisit our high school wardrobes.) No, what I'm looking for are the inner traits—attitude, language, and exterior reflections of the heart.

In our home, Sue and I carefully monitor the friends our kids spend time with. We pay close attention to the attitudes that come home with our children after spending time at a friend's house. If we notice a problem developing, we curtail the time they're able to spend with that friend. We have an agreement, based on Proverbs 12:26, with our six kids: They prove to us that their friendships are worthwhile, or we help them find new friendships that are.

BUSY PARENTS AND THEIR CHILD'S FRIENDS

None of us need to be reminded how busy we are. Trying to balance work, family, church, and other responsibilities is difficult in our modern-day, frenetic culture. As someone has said, "Life is a rat race, and the rats are winning!"

As parents we are just plain busy—sometimes too busy to properly guide our children into positive friendships. The wise parent keeps close watch on his child and the friends he or she is choosing to be with. Some might say, "Come on, I trust my children to make wise decisions. I don't want to meddle in their business."

Parents, please meddle! Get as involved as you can in picking their friends, then do a little more. Especially during their younger years, don't be seduced into giving them freedoms for which they're not ready. I encourage parents to follow this rule: Never allow your children to go to a house where you don't know the parents. Never. This is especially true if the parents are not home at the time. This is doubly important when it comes to spending the night at a friend's house. Our kids may go to a sleepover only if we know the parents well. No exceptions. If our child feels we're being unfair, we say, "OK, why don't you invite so-and-so over here. That way we can get to know him, and we'll all have a great time together."

Unless your child is compliant to a fault, chances are he won't be happy to turn his social calendar over to Mom and Dad, especially when he reaches high school age. So what does a parent do? Here are a few ideas that might work in guiding children's friendships.

PRAY FOR GODLY RELATIONSHIPS

This is more than a token spiritual prerequisite. Consistent, prevailing prayer for our children is crucial if we're to see them follow Christ and stay pure in our current society. Though we need to pray for their spiritual welfare in all areas, the issue of proper relationships needs to be right at the top of your prayer list.

ASK ABOUT THEIR FRIENDS

We always ask our kids about their friends. We'll chat about what they do and don't appreciate about the choices their friends make. Sometimes I hear things about people I'd rather not hear. As a pastor and a parent, it pains me to know that some of their acquaintances are fooling around with alcohol or are involved in premarital sex. We don't encourage them to gossip, but we do listen carefully to gauge the reaction of our children to what they see around them. However, we're finding that if we overreact to what they say, it's over; from that point on, we'll never hear anything but positive things about their friends.

Parents, maybe you've found, as we have, that bedtime can be a powerful time to connect with your kids. There's something about the day winding down and the head hitting the pillow that can relax tensions between parent and child. We try to take advantage of these times—we know we won't have them forever. Sometimes I'll sit on my kids' beds and rub their feet or shoulders and not say anything. The important thing is that we're there—protecting them, listening to them, comforting them, identifying with them. These simple moments go a long way toward knitting our hearts together.

HELP THEM CHOOSE

Over the years, we've learned to take an active role in helping our kids choose friends, especially if we see them struggling in this area. For instance, we might say, "How's so-and-so doing?"

"Fine," they would say.

"Hey," I'd reply, "let's call him up and go to a movie together."

"OK, Dad, let's go."

A gentle encouragement in the right direction can go a long way. Awhile back I noticed that a couple of the students in our high school ministry were starting to drift in their walk with Christ. Nothing too obvious, only indications they weren't doing well. We began to invite them over to the house to hang out with our family. When parents do this, it's actually a double investment in the future: We're helping our kids choose healthy friendships, and we also get to influence other kids in their walk with Christ.

GET TO KNOW THEIR FRIENDS

My wife and I have determined to know more about our child's friends than merely seeing them walk from our front door to our kid's room. If our knowledge about the friend is limited, we'll be limited in our discernment. When friends come over to the house, we make it a practice to sit down with them. We get to know them, ask questions, and joke around. Never think that your child wants you completely out of the way; he may need his space, but never leave him completely to himself.

I can influence these young people by intruding into their lives. Parents, don't you love it when another adult has a positive influence on your child? Our children have had the benefit of many godly, adult role models, and we're forever thankful to each of them. We want to do the same for their kids; it's great when parents help each other in this way.

As we get to know our kid's friends, we also get to know their habits. Let's say one of my son's friends consistently drives his car eighty miles per hour. Chances are, if I'm close enough to my kids, I'll know that. So I'll casually put this friend in a headlock (playing around, of course) and say, "Joe, I hear you're driving kind of fast; if you keep that up I'm going to kick your rear!" I do it in a joking way, but he knows I'm serious about the speed!

We work hard to make our house a place where kids want to hang out: lots of food and lots of fun! Is it inconvenient? Almost always—but it's well worth it, for our kids' sake. Your students and their friends will love it. The key is involvement. Some parents come across like police officers, minus only the badge. This kind of parenting is all law and no grace. No wonder some kids would rather be anywhere than at home. Although I'm not afraid to enforce our family rules, I prefer the role of teacher, coach, and influencer.

Don't Ignore Warning Signals

So how do we know when a certain friendship is unhealthy for our child? Here are a few warning signals:

Isolation and Noncommunication

Teenagers want to be independent; didn't you at that age? As parents, our job description includes preparing our kids for life on their own (Prov. 3:1–2). There is a "launch-date" on the horizon, whether we want to admit it or not. Thus, the wise parent looks for ways to instill a healthy confidence in the child, so that good decision making becomes a natural way of life. A slow, premeditated loosening of the apron strings is not only healthy, but also entirely necessary as a child grows to adulthood.

Students, however, want their independence all at once. At least, they say they do. One caution for parents in this area: Don't lengthen the leash too soon. A certain amount of independence is normal and healthy, but too much slack on the parent's part may lead to unintended consequences. It's easier to let out the leash slowly than to have to reel it back in.

I know of a family that struggled with one of their junior high daughters when she began hanging around a popular crew of girls. The daughter began to develop an independent attitude. She began to exhibit traits of her friends' homes, rather than the attitude of her own home.

Without trying to create distrust, these parents watched her friendships very closely. These kids were not getting into drugs or immorality, but they had a "loose" spirit—in other words, a sense of unhealthy independence.

In this case, the family decided to take the daughter out of the situation by homeschooling her for a year to remove her from unhealthy influences. Thankfully, it paid off. The next year she was back in public school and did extremely well, both in choosing friends and in her walk with Christ. These parents stopped their daughter from going where the crowd was headed. Now, the girl sees that many friends from the old crowd have continued down the path they started in junior high, with tragic consequences. She's thankful for her parents' intervention.

Another example is John, a father who noticed his daughter's attitude at home was changing for the worse. She was hanging out with students who were influencing her in ways he recognized as destructive. The difficulty, however, was in convincing his wife that something was wrong. She lacked discernment about choices the daughter was making. The mom was trying to be her girl's friend and enjoyed the fact that popular young men were pursuing her daughter, even though they were not believers. John and I met together, and I said, "Friend, you need to lead your home and step in, or you will lose your daughter." He did it; he stepped in, took control, and saved his girl from a lot of pain.

Of course, the daughter wasn't happy that Dad gently took control of some aspects of her social life. She complained to Mom, but both parents held their ground and didn't budge. Now, after years have passed, this daughter sees the wisdom of John's actions. She's thankful for his leadership, even though it seemed tough at the time. Best of all, she is now living with a renewed passion for Christ.

This gets to the heart of isolation and noncommunication on the part of our children. Parents, ask yourself this question: "If you treated your friends the way you treat your kids, would your friends want to spend time with you?" From what I've observed, many kids who isolate themselves from their parents do so because it's not enjoyable to be at home. Certainly that's not the only reason, but it bears close examination. An atmosphere of acceptance, affirmation, and fun at home goes a long way toward keeping our children from seeking these things elsewhere.

COVERING UP A FRIEND'S WRONG CHOICES

Every one of us is tempted to overlook the sin in our lives. We love to make excuses for our failures, and students are no different. They will, however, often cover up their friends' wrongdoings, if only because they want to be accepted by them. If we're not careful, this can escalate into an "us versus them" debate, in which their friends are always right and we, the parents, are always wrong.

It's understandable that our children want to be loyal. In fact, we should encourage them to be. But help your child understand what loyalty means. Loyalty doesn't mean turning a blind eye to evil; a good friend will seek God's best for the other. Find teachable moments (e.g., bedtime or driving in the car) and casually bring up stories about the friends you had while growing up. (Your kids love to hear stories, especially about your growing-up years.) Tell them about students you know who made wise decisions, and some who didn't. Let them know that you, too, struggled with friendships when you were their age. Don't preach at them—coach them. Tell them stories about misplaced loyalty, when you or others were loyal to people or things that didn't deserve your allegiance. Help them establish their own guardrails in this area of friendship.

A wise parent will point out a friend's wrong behavior yet not attack the friend outright. Let the behavior be the issue at hand; otherwise your child will likely become defensive and side with the friend no matter what! It's better to say, "Honey, I don't like the attitude I see in your friend," than to say, "Honey, I don't like your friend. His attitude stinks!" You may not like the friend at all, but how you frame your words may determine whether or not your child defends ungodly behavior.

However, not every "imperfect" friendship should be discouraged. Our son Ben had a friend who would say disrespectful things, even at our house. He was a good kid, but he struggled with a poor attitude. I said to Ben, "I like this kid, but I don't like his disrespectful mouth." By affirming his friend, I was also affirming Ben and his ability to choose friends. But I was letting Ben know we saw a problem.

Kids go through seasons of life, as we do. Ben's friend eventually matured in attitude and respect. Now this same friend is very respectful. Don't be overly critical; we can't boot every kid out the door, nor would we want to. The truth is, we'll see things we don't like in most every kid who befriends our children. Other parents will see things in our kids too. We need to allow students the freedom to mature over time.

But what if your kid is hanging with real trouble? Not merely normal adolescent behavior, but hard-core stuff: drugs, drinking, blasphemy, and lawlessness? First, I'd kick myself in the rear for allowing it to happen in the first place. Then I'd let the friend who is a poor influence know he's on my bad side, in no uncertain terms. I would clearly tell my child the things I don't appreciate about the friend's behavior and would do whatever I could to curtail their opportunities to be together. This would be a time for serious prayer and counsel. If your children enjoy hanging out with people who party, drink, and do drugs, you'll need to watch them very carefully. Just the fact that they're attracted to kids in that lifestyle is a strong warning signal.

Harmful Family Influences

Another way to direct your child's friendships is by spending time with families you respect. Kids' lives are deeply enriched when they see other parents who hold similar values. Families help each other out when they do this, especially when their kids are similar in age. Doing fun things together as families, such as camping, waterskiing, and hiking, can be enriching in many ways.

Of course, not all homes share our convictions. One of my sons has a friend who is Mormon. He's a good kid from a wonderful family, and we enjoy having him spend time at our house. However, because of the major theological differences we have with Mormonism, I'm careful to talk to my son about doctrine. We've had great discussions. Though the moral values of our two homes are similar, our theological views are extremely different. I've found that overreacting or being critical of others doesn't help; instead, I want to implant a vision in my son to reach his friend for Christ.

My son can look at his friend's family and say, "Dad, what's wrong with Mormonism? They are nice people, have good morals, and they say they believe the Bible." I affirm these things, but then help him understand the heretical views concerning the nature of God, the person of Jesus Christ, and many other Mormon doctrines. I help him discern not only moral issues but theological truths as well. I don't discourage their friendship, but it's important my son is aware of what his friend believes. Of course, I'm never personally critical toward his friend's family. Though there are major differences theologically, there's also a strong mutual respect. This, too, is a part of mentoring our kids—we want them to be respectful in the midst of disagreement.

FRIENDSHIPS WITH OLDER KIDS

One of the greatest needs our young people experience is that of being accepted by their peer group, by people their own age. A whole different level of acceptance is reached, however, when students begin hanging out with older friends. Many parents wonder if there's any harm in their child having older kids as their best friends.

There are things to be very aware of in older-younger friendships. Usually, older kids have more freedom and interpret life differently than those who are younger. In many cases an age difference of a few years can mean a huge gap in terms of innocence and life experience. When I was in school, I had a friend who was a couple of years older than me. Looking back on our relationship, I now understand I was exposed to a level of life that I shouldn't have been at that age. His interests were different from mine, his body more mature, his mind aware of things that were new to me. He wasn't a bad person, only older. Be careful, unless your child's friend is a quality kid from a quality family. I have no problem with older kids mentoring my student, but I don't want them becoming best friends.

Years ago, one of our high school leaders befriended a student who was several years younger. Actually, this leader was in his midtwenties, while the student was a sophomore in high school. At first, the leader was nothing more than a mentor, but after awhile he began to pursue the younger student as a best friend. The leader had his own apartment and his own car. He began to come over to the boy's house and pick him up to do things together. For the high schooler it was a big thrill. Here was a friend with real independence—an adult—who wanted to spend time with him. It became easy, however, for the boy to forget the reasons why he shouldn't have the same level of independence his older friend was enjoying. That's not unusual—the younger person often feels he deserves the same freedoms as the older friend, when in reality he's too young to handle the responsibility.

The young boy's family ended up discouraging this relationship. The leader had begun to undermine the family's authority and overtly questioned the young man's boundaries. Clearly, he had become an unhealthy influence in this student's life. From what I've seen, this is typical of older-younger friendships. Yes, there are exceptions to the rule. Girls, who are more mature relationally, may be able to hang out with older girls without being affected negatively. Still, caution is in order.

The challenge here is to examine every friendship carefully: Is it healthy for your child's spiritual life? Is it detrimental to the same-age relationships she already enjoys? Is it increasing her awareness of things best discovered at an older age? Is it making her wrongfully dissatisfied with her current level of independence and freedom? These are issues to be aware of in older-younger friendships.

NON-CHRISTIAN FRIENDS AND UNHEALTHY FRIENDSHIPS

Over the years I've seen hundreds of Christian students who've done well in the area of friendships. None of us can live the Christian life alone, nor are we meant to. But when Christian students choose non-Christians as their closest friends, it's difficult for them to stay single-minded. Second Corinthians 6:14 tells us, "Do not be mismatched with unbelievers. For what partnership is there between righteousness and lawlessness? Or what fellowship does light have with darkness?" It's my conviction that students should have both Christian and non-Christian friends. However, their best friends need to be students who love Christ.

One young man in our ministry, a star athlete, was very well known on his high school campus. But instead of hanging out with only the most popular people, he chose to be friends with other Christians, popular or not. He knew that healthy friendships would encourage him to keep following Christ. He worked to remain matched with believing students.

Students who don't make friends easily are those most susceptible to unhealthy friendships. They're often starved for attention and will open themselves up to bad influences. Unfortunately, the drug groups are often the easiest to break into on most campuses. These groups are very accepting— anyone who will join them in their behavior is welcome. If your student has a hard time making friends, for whatever reason, pray diligently that God will send a positive friend or two. You probably can't change your child's social aptitudes, so don't get angry with him. Instead, help him be aware of the dangers of poor friendships. Involve him in activities in which he can shine, and do your best to surround him with positive influences.

Every student desires to have friends. If your child has a hard time socially, it's very difficult on both her and you. I remember one girl in our ministry who fabricated stories to gain attention. One evening her friends brought her to my office, and she told me she'd been raped and was now pregnant. The story went on for awhile until, when pressed, the girl finally admitted she'd been telling a lie. She yearned to have close friends but didn't know how to make them or keep them. Sadly, she used deceit and played the victim as a means of gaining attention.

Sometimes parents relive their own adolescence through their child's social life. For instance, some moms encourage their daughters to be in a certain social group, even if the girls couldn't care less. It can lead Mom to gossip about other girls and their families. By doing this, they teach their daughters how to do the same. Of course, dads can do similar things with their sons. It happens when parents remember the pains of their youth and then zealously try to protect their kids from the same ordeals. A better approach, however, is to mentor our kids through difficulties, rather than automatically seeking to intervene.

POOR SPIRITUAL INDICATORS

Nothing is more important to us as Christian parents than to see our students love and obey Jesus Christ. It's our highest goal and our greatest aspiration as we reflect on the responsibility of raising children. It almost goes without saying, then, that we as Christian parents must be on the lookout for any influences that would detract from our child's spiritual walk. But how do we gauge the spiritual impact of a child's friends? How do we accurately assess a child's spiritual temperature?

Every person trained in medicine knows to check the vital signs when confronted with a medical emergency. Pulse, breathing, heart rate, temperature, and blood pressure are signs of life. They help the paramedic, nurse, or doctor quickly determine the medical condition of the person in need.

In Galatians 5 we find a list of spiritual vital signs. When the items on this list are present in the life of an individual, it's a good indication the Holy Spirit has invaded that soul and is slowly beginning to dominate his attitudes, actions, and lifestyle. If a child is growing in Christ, there will be evidence of the Holy Spirit's presence, as found in Galatians 5:22–23: love, joy, peace, patience, kindness, goodness, faith, gentleness, and self-control.

Do you see these qualities developing in the life of your child and in her friends? Not that we should be unrealistic in our expectations—kids go through incredible changes as their bodies mature. Raging hormones can create enormous mood swings, and peer pressure often sweeps over young lives with hurricane-level intensity. Sometimes our kids make foolish choices; it's helpful if we remember how much we ourselves have learned by way of wrong decisions. Still, if there is spiritual life, it will evidence itself by the fruit of the Spirit, even if in seed form.

The opposite attributes are found in the preceding verses. Here is the list of "works of the flesh" as described in Galatians 5:19–21: "Now the works of the flesh are obvious:

sexual immorality, moral impurity, promiscuity, idolatry, sorcery, hatreds, strife, jealousy, outbursts of anger, selfish ambitions, dissensions, factions, envy, drunkenness, carousing, and anything similar, about which I tell you in advance—as I told you before—that those who practice such things will not inherit the kingdom of God."

Obviously, this is a checklist of things none of us want to see in our children. Many of us know from experience this kind of fruit has a very bitter aftertaste! Parents, if your child's friendships are producing or encouraging these types of behaviors, do whatever is in your power to discourage the relationship. Don't just say to yourself, "It's OK. This is normal teenager stuff." Sin is never normal for the child of God. We all know how challenging adolescence can be, but be careful not to excuse ungodly behavior as if it were a rite of passage!

Conclusion

If your child finds herself in a social class you don't approve of, try not to become frustrated. If you want her to be an athlete and she can't throw a ball, or a musician and she can't carry a tune, it's OK. Help her find good friends both inside and outside her natural associations. Remember, you can set the tone when it comes to her choice of friends. Ask God for wisdom, then seek ways to be involved. Wise parents will make this a priority as they influence the next generation for Christ.

CHAPTER SEVEN

Influencing Your Kid's Friends for Christ

It's one thing to have a vision for your child—it's a step further to have a vision for your child's friends. Imagine if every

[...]luence his child's peers
[...] the students who come
[...]g in the lives of our kids
[...]g that God can use us in
[...]ake it happen.

[...]in the Bible is the story
[...]ed great things for God.
[...]vas the son of the first
[...]hepherd boy chosen by
[...]. Both young men had
[...]t roles to play in Israel's
[...]on more than just com-
[...]ual friendship—a God-

[...]l 18, it strikes me that
[...]sition. In fact, quite the

opposite—they ended up rooting for each other. Think for a moment of what Jonathan was giving up by helping his friend David. Jonathan was heir to the throne, yet he humbled himself and worked to see his best friend become king instead. Jonathan wanted what God wanted, rather than the desires of his own flesh.

David, too, showed unflinching loyalty to his friend Jonathan. He could have tried to divide Jonathan from his father, causing a split in the kingdom. Yet David did nothing of the sort. He, too, humbled himself and protected Jonathan from having to choose between him and his father. David could have said, "Me or your dad—make your choice!"

When I think of the friendship these two men shared, I gain a picture of what God-centered friendships are like for our students. I believe many of our children are up to the challenge. Many believing students in this current generation are attracted to life on the edge. This means when they decide to live for Christ, they're not kidding. But they very rarely will do it alone. As parents, we can help our kids by encouraging them into Jonathan-David type relationships. When students have God-centered friendships with others their own age, watch out!

For instance, students love stories about people who've died for their faith. The reason? They get a picture of what God can do through them and their friends; their hearts are set ablaze. I've had students tell me they're ready to die for Christ. But rarely will they attempt to do great things for God all by themselves. Their commitment is heightened within the context of friendships.

I think of two guys named Zach and Tony as an example. These two students decided they wanted to make an impact on their high school campus. Both of them were popular because of their involvement in sports and other activities. After discussing ideas and praying about their options, they made up T-shirts that said, "I agree with Zach and Tony." They then gave the shirts to their Christian friends, who wore them at school. When students would see the shirts and ask, "Why do you agree with Zach and Tony?" they would hear the answer, "Come to a meeting Thursday night and find out."

As you can imagine, the level of curiosity on campus was intense. That Thursday evening more than one hundred students attended. This gave Zach, Tony, and their friends the opportunity to share the gospel. What an incredible experience, but notice they didn't work independently. It was two friends, with a larger community, who together "promote[d] love and good works" (Heb. 10:24).

The story behind the story is this: Both young men will tell you their parents have had a tremendous influence in their lives. These parents stayed involved in their boys' spiritual walk, and their influence remained strong as the boys went through high school.

When kids in this emerging generation get zealous for Christ, they become incredibly hungry for God's Word. As their pastor, I often feel pressure to keep up with them in their zeal. They keep me sharp because of their intense hunger to learn more about God.

One time my son Ben brought home a couple of friends I'd never seen before, so I sat down on the couch and started chatting with them. "So, where do you guys go to church?" I asked.

"Well, we don't really go to church very often," was the reply.

"Well, how long have you guys known the Lord?" I continued.

"Not very long," they said. "We're new at this. Actually, we've been smoking pot for quite awhile, and we're trying to stop."

I thought to myself, *Oh, crud. These guys are fresh out of it. I need to watch this relationship.* So that's what I did. I made sure that if Ben was going to hang out with these guys, we would influence them for good rather than the other way around. Ben and I started a weekly Bible study with them both and enjoyed watching them get excited about Christ. It was great.

After a couple of years, these two young men were so strong and zealous for Christ that they decided, on their own, to stand on their high school campus and hand out gospel tracts. One of the boys ended up bringing his grandmother to church, and she came to know the Lord. Both of them went on to Bible school, and now one of them is preparing for full-time ministry. Ben and I were just a small part of God's plan. God used us because we felt we could make a difference in their lives.

Making It Work

How do we go about influencing our children's friends for the Lord? Here are practical ideas that seem to work well. First, try having spontaneous conversations with students who come to your house. Don't preach at them but be natural and attentive. For instance, one of my son's friends, a new believer, had come to visit. I came up to him and put him in a playful headlock, saying, "Hey, guy, you're gonna stay strong with Jesus, right? You're not gonna pull away from Christ, are you?"

"Oh no, Mr. Keels. I would never do that," he replied. He knows I love him to pieces, and that I'm serious about him staying strong in the Lord. Yet doing it in a playful way keeps it from getting too heavy.

Get to know your child's friends by sitting down and talk-ing with them. Remember, if you make it a big deal, it will backfire. As you get to know them over time, ask questions that reveal where they're at spiritually. You can ask things like, "Where do you go to church?" or "How long have you been a Christian?" There are times when your kids may be embar-rassed to have you talk about spiritual things in front of oth-ers. They may say, "Dad," or roll their eyes and say, "Mom, what are you doing?" You don't have to explain your strategy to your kids. As Nike says, "Just do it." But don't be over-bearing—don't push too much. Look for openings to build into their lives. If your child is used to hearing you talk about Christ in the home, chances are it won't be a big deal when you do so with his friends.

If, however, your son or daughter gets angry, you should probably back off. Try a different tack or just put it on the back burner for awhile. You don't want to damage the rela-tionship with your child by pushing too hard with his friends. In fact, it may be that the most powerful influence you have in his friends' lives is that of being a loving example, nothing more. Some of your kid's friends won't want to hang around you—period. Be flexible, be open, and be attentive to what the Lord may be doing in that young person's life. But always be sensitive to your own child as well.

If you know your son's or daughter's friends well, you might consider inviting them to your house before Monday Night Football for a question-and-answer time regarding the Bible. In some cases, you won't need to ask your child's per-mission to do so. Just invite the friends, provide lots of food and soft drinks, and go for it.

My own life story illustrates the incredible impact of a friend's parents. I came to Christ because a great Christian guy, Dave Smith, decided to hang out with me. This was during my high school days, before I'd given my life to Christ. Dave and I spent time at his house, and I was intrigued by how his parents talked so freely about the Lord. Dave would just sit back and smile as he watched his mom talk to me about what she was learning in her Bible studies at church. Dave's dad was a scientist, and he would tell me about the fallacies of evolution and how modern science gave evidence for God's existence. I'd sit there and say, "Really? I've never heard *that* before."

The Smith's were the first real Christian family I'd ever spent much time with. I was amazed at how real they were and how much they allowed God to be a part of their lives. As I look back on it, these were the people who led me to Christ. I'll never forget their impact on my life.

Maybe this is the reason I have such a passion for all Christian parents to do the same. I know it works—I myself am exhibit A. Imagine if every Christian parent took this seriously. Imagine us not being scared of unbelievers but actually teaching our kids to love people into the Kingdom. Ninety percent of individuals who accept Christ as Savior do so before their eighteenth birthday. Our sons and daughters enter a bountiful mission field every day when they head off to school. How might the Lord use you to reach some of these students for Christ?

Dads, some of you will be like a second father to students who are being raised by single moms. Many kids need good adult role models, and they don't have them at home. Moms, too, consider the impact you can have on your daughter's friends. You can influence entire families by loving and mentoring even one student.

WHAT IF MY KID IS EMBARRASSED?

Teenagers have a way of letting us know when we embarrass them, don't they? Certainly, we have to be sensitive to our own kids as we seek to influence their friends. Yet as we've said before, this generation will allow parents to influence them in ways previous generations might not have. I think of the proverb that says, "the pride of sons is their fathers" (Prov. 17:6b). Our kids really do want to be proud of us, though they'll often try to hide this fact. Whenever I talk to a kid about his parents and pay them a compliment, I can see the student's chest puff out. Kids long to be proud of their parents.

For example, when my youngest son, Jason, was just five or six years old, he came up to me one day and asked me to flex my muscles. I complied but only for his sake, of course. He wrapped his little hands over them and said, "Wow, Dad, they're huge." Then he got real serious for a moment before saying, "Dad, do you think you could whip Arnold Schwarzenegger?"

I leaned down close to his ear, and after looking around the room to make sure no one else could hear, I said "Yep!"

A serious look of satisfaction settled on his face. "I thought so," he said, and walked away. For that moment, at least, everything was OK in his little world.

Don't expect your teenagers to rave about your attributes in quite the same way. Still, they have that same desire to be proud of their parents. Dads, this is especially true for your sons. They long to take pride in your masculinity and strength.

WHOM DO I MENTOR?

I find it interesting just how many parents believe that the church youth group is primarily responsible for mentoring the next generation. Granted, student ministries exist to assist young people and their families. But in my view, and I believe it's biblical, the weight of responsibility for raising kids is on the parents.

I've had parents say to me, "I really feel a burden to minister to young teenage girls. Do you have a group I can disciple?" I'll often respond, "Why not disciple the young gals that are your daughter's friends? Just start there." This may not always work, but why not give it a try? Many of us parents don't bat an eye at inviting complete strangers to our house for a small-group Bible study, but when it comes to actively influencing our kids' friends for the Lord, we break out in a cold sweat.

I understand this concept will be challenging for many who read this book. It's difficult to influence our own children for the Lord, let alone the friends they bring home. As you read this, you may be tempted to blow it off and give any of twenty-nine excuses why it will never work. Instead, I encourage you to go ahead with prayer and resolve to make it happen. Mentoring may not look the same for you as it does for me, but by God's strength we can have an incredible impact on those students who hang around our kids. By doing so, we'll be modeling a love for both God and people who will remain with our children the rest of their lives.

STEPS FOR STARTING A BIBLE STUDY

First, develop a heart for the students who hang around your kids. Reject a critical spirit and instead be thinking about the potential in each life. Have a vision for helping your children develop Jonathan-David relationships with their peers.

Second, be ready with questions that will act as conversation starters. You might consider reading the *TQ Survival Guide*, which covers doctrinal material by way of stories and teaching. Also, the *TQ Study Bible* contains thought-provoking questions on each page and is useful for helping students become engaged with the text.

Third, have lots of food available and keep things relaxed. It's better to have a shorter study that's meaningful, than a long study that's boring. Also, let them see that you're learning, too, and that God's Word is incredibly exciting.

Fourth, be careful of lecturing. Nobody wants to be bored to death. Girls have the advantage here, for they can more naturally keep a conversation going. Leading guys in a study is a challenge and generally requires more preparation on the part of the leader.

So why not dive in and give it a try? Who knows how God might use you in the lives of your kids' friends.

CHAPTER EIGHT

The Pain
of a Rebellious Child

Most of my children have a stubborn streak, which I imagine they inherited from me. Can you relate to this with any of your kids? I love the fact that they're strong willed, but this means extra energy is required to keep them from developing a rebellious spirit.

A number of years ago one of my sons decided it was easier to sleep in his clothes than take them off before going to bed. This wasn't a huge deal, but it meant he would then get up and go to school in clothes that were rumpled and wrinkled. When I noticed this, I called him on it and said, "Don't crawl into the sheets with your clothes on, OK, son?" His response was less than thrilling. "No, Dad. I want to." Of course, now I was seeing not just rumpled clothes but an attitude that needed to be dealt with.

I knew I had to win the war, or it would come back to bite me later. I said, "Son, you're going to get out of those clothes right now." It was a battle, but he finally took his clothes off and got into bed. By then he was steaming mad, and he lashed out by saying, "You know what? I hate you." Believe me, some good responses came to my mind at that moment. I felt like saying, "Well, right now I'm not too fond of you either." I was angry at what he'd said, and I told him his words had crossed the line before letting him go to bed: "Hate speech is unacceptable."

He was still pouting the next morning. I think he must've been enjoying it, otherwise he would've apologized and gone on with life. But I wasn't about to let it go. At the breakfast table I rehearsed with him what had happened the previous evening. I let him feel some of my intensity; he needed to see that a rebellious attitude was not allowed.

After breakfast he walked over to Sue and said, "Mother, I'm sorry." Then he turned around and walked right past me. It's obvious he wasn't sorry, he was just jumping through some hoops. On the way to school that morning, he was told that his poor attitude would result in an early bedtime that evening and that he wasn't to go outside and play after school. I was determined that he understand the depth of his poor attitude and that he feel the consequences of his actions.

By that afternoon, his heart hadn't changed; his poor attitude was still in control. We spent time talking about the fact that his problem was a heart issue, and that if it wasn't dealt with it would recur again and again. Still, he refused to listen, and it was off to bed at an early hour.

The next morning I finally saw his spirit soften, and we talked about how things had gone from bad to worse. He realized that the situation had escalated from poor behavior to a rebellious attitude. He leaned over and said, "Daddy, I'm really sorry for what I did." I could see it in his eyes—he really was sorry, and it was written all over his face. The tears began to fall, and then we were buddies again.

CATCH IT EARLY

It was a difficult couple of days in our household but worth it. It's not that he will never show a rebellious attitude again. I'm sure we'll go through many similar experiences in the future. But the fact is, if rebellion gets out of control at a young age, it usually gets worse over time. It must be confronted, and parents need to make sure they win when it shows its ugly head. Sometimes we hate the pain of confrontation so much that we won't deal with rebellion until it's undeniable. Instead, I encourage parents to notice the signs and pay attention without overreacting. Never give up dealing with what is clearly a rebellious attitude.

Left unchecked, a rebellious attitude will destroy your home. After many years of observing students, I can honestly say that parents need to have a proper fear of rebellion. I wish I could say that Christian families are exempt from this kind of pain, but it's not true. Many good families have experienced the bitter fruit of a child's rebellious choices. Even great parents can find themselves dealing with a rebellious teenager.

I hate having to discipline my kids; I've never known a parent who enjoys it. But in order to stay on top of rebellion, I know there are times when discipline is needed (Heb. 12:11). Of course, sometimes things don't go as planned, like the time one of my boys, then eight years old, knew he deserved a spanking. He saw me coming with the paddle and immediately ran upstairs to his room. I followed him up and said, "OK, buddy, time for your swat." But as I looked at him I saw that his rear end was huge—he'd stuffed the backside of his pants with extra clothes so the spanking wouldn't hurt. He looked so ridiculous standing there with his lumpy backside sticking out that I couldn't help but start laughing.

Soon we were both giggling so hard I couldn't have swatted him if I'd tried.

Rebellion is to be avoided at all costs, but there are no guarantees that it won't happen in your family. None of us can stop our kids from doing stupid things, and ultimately we can't live their lives for them. I never tell a parent, "If you just do these five things, your kids will turn out great." Sue and I learned this the hard way. One of our older boys would always keep us on our knees. When he hit adolescence, he'd sometimes say to me, "Dad, I'm thinking I'd like to go to parties."

Inside I was dying, and I wanted to give him fifteen lectures to set him straight. What didn't help was the negative attitude we got from some of our friends. When they saw our son's wandering eyes, they made it clear they thought we weren't doing well as parents. In my mind I could hear them saying, "Well, Steve, if you only had your boy memorize more Bible verses, or go to church more, or . . ." It drove me nuts. My son wasn't taking off and doing drugs, but his eyes were heading in the wrong direction.

I know that parents will handle this differently, but this is what I did. One day my son and I were talking about hell, and I told him that when he was a toddler, I would put him on my shoulders and pray for him as we walked under the stars. I told him about the times I'd told the Lord that if my son ever stopped walking with Him that He might as well take my boy to heaven early. Perhaps my prayers were overzealous, but the story had its intended impact on my son. He said, "Oh, great. Thanks a lot, Dad." Somehow, it made him understand that following God is serious business.

Let's face it, your kids aren't perfect and neither are mine. They'll often say or do things that are immature and just plain stupid. They may even act in ways contrary to the values by which they've been raised. I don't classify every sassy moment or every bad choice as rebellion. Some kids have a good heart yet have a knack for getting into trouble. Normal kids make normal mistakes. What concerns me, however, are students who have a defiant heart. These are the kids who will stare you in the face and, without blinking an eye, refuse to obey. This defiance and an unteachable heart need to be handled firmly yet lovingly. These students require a great amount of attention from their parents.

For certain kids rebellion becomes an addiction. Just as some people become addicted to pornography or drugs, in the same way rebellion can take hold in a person's heart. There are students who find enjoyment in a rebellious attitude, and when they do, it becomes difficult for them to change. They so crave independence that they ignore their own best interests and those of their family. These kids will hear how much you love them but don't easily feel the strength of your love. Of course, this can be traumatic for us as parents. If someone else's kid is rebellious, it probably won't keep you up at night. But when your child is acting out, you'll be the one who's tossing and turning all night long.

Sadly, rebellion can show up in even the strongest homes. Some families have a number of kids who do well, and one who decides to follow a rebellious path. The effect on parents is tangible—I've had moms tell me their insides feel as if they're hollowed out because of the pain. It always grieves me when I become aware of these situations, and I give these parents a lot of grace. When rebellion comes into a home, it can feel like the pain of death.

I find it especially difficult to observe dads when their daughters rebel. A dad pretty much knows what to do with a boy who's making wrong choices; Dad feels he can be somewhat forceful. He basically understands how to relate to his son, for he remembers being a young male adolescent. But with daughters, dads often feel helpless. They can become panicky and reserved, and then sometimes explode in anger. All they see is their baby girl pushing them away, and it's a helpless feeling.

My point in showing this ugly side of rebellion is to encourage parents to deal with it early. We don't want to overreact at every little sign of disobedience. But a defiant and rebellious attitude must be confronted. It takes time and effort, but the alternative is often very painful.

Signs of Rebellion

What does rebellion look like? What are some of the early signs a child is heading in that direction? Here are what I call the seeds of rebellion. Please don't be alarmed—many of these seeds are common in adolescents. Parents should be concerned, however, when one, or more, of these traits becomes a habit, a regular occurrence. If you notice a trait beginning to take hold in your son or daughter, make sure you keep your eye on it, and do what you can to keep it from bearing the fruit of full-blown rebellion (Gal. 5:22–23).

Telling Lies

This is an early indicator of a rebellious spirit. In fact, deception is at the very heart of rebellion. In some kids, lying and deceit can become such a habit they actually begin to believe some of their own stories.

There are few things more painful than realizing your child has been lying to you. All sense of trust is immediately destroyed. It's hard to believe that the sweet little cherub you so lovingly raised could now look you in the face and blatantly distort the truth. It's difficult when a parent finds his child has been sneaking out of the house or doing wrong things behind his back. Most kids desire to have the trust of their parents. Thus, a telltale sign of rebellion is when a student doesn't care if he has his parents' trust.

Some of our kids become very good at telling us what we want to hear. Having been raised in the church, they can speak "Christian-ese." They may allay our concerns when, in fact, there's plenty going on we don't know about. Students who do this will usually find friends who deceive their parents in the same way. You can imagine how difficult it becomes to trust a child mired in this kind of deception.

WITHDRAWAL FROM THE FAMILY

During adolescence a natural process of withdrawal takes place. Students are becoming adults, and there needs to be a gradual loosening of the apron strings as they learn to make decisions on their own. This is normal. It's not normal, however, for a student to withdraw from the family for extended periods of time. For instance, a child may come home from school, lock herself in her bedroom, and stay there for hours without coming out. This kind of withdrawal keeps her from relating to family members, and makes it easy for her to develop her own values apart from the family system. The more she's isolated, the bigger the rift that can develop between her and the rest of the family.

I encourage parents to get her out of her room and into the family room or wherever the rest of the family is gathered. Of course, she'll complain by saying, "This is stupid." Merely say, "That's OK. Sit here and have a stupid time on the couch. Isn't it great? You don't have to do anything but sit here and be with us." Do your best, however, to not let her sour spirit create a melancholy home. Keep her with you, but don't let her bad attitude destroy family time.

Related to isolation is the whole subject of the Internet and the use of online chat rooms. If a student has an Internet-connected computer in her room, parents need to be especially careful to monitor the sites she visits and the people with whom she chats. My personal view is that any computer with online access must be out in open spaces, such as in the family room. This way anyone can walk by and see what's online. Also, the time a child spends online and in chat rooms should be limited. These things can become addictive for our kids, and parents can't afford to believe that our kids are beyond getting into trouble online.

Though some will disagree with me, I believe parents have the right to invade their kids' privacy. In fact, I say it's an obligation. I tell my kids that as long as they live under my roof, I have full right to go through their rooms and look at whatever I find. There's too much at stake not to do so.

Fascination with a Culture of Rebellion

When visiting families, there are times when I've gone into the bedrooms of Christian students and been surprised at what I find. I've seen Ouija boards and posters of heavy-metal bands, scantily clad models, and foulmouthed athletes. The room reflects a different culture from the rest of the house. We should never allow our child's room to breed a culture of rebellion.

We sometimes forget the influence that popular musicians and athletes have in our cultures. Our children are surrounded by a media blitz that can overwhelm them with images, attitudes, and worldviews antithetical to what we believe. Why do parents allow lewd posters in their students' rooms or filthy music to blare from the stereo? Sometimes parents don't want to come down hard as their own parents did; they want to have an open spirit. In so doing, they allow things into their child's lives that are contrary to the Bible. This can't help but have a negative impact on their children's spiritual lives.

The Goth culture is another example of rebellion. These are the kids that dress in black, spike their hair, and appear to have a collective preoccupation with death. At its root it's anti-God and antiauthority. If your son or daughter is adopting this kind of look and attitude, do whatever it takes to get them away from it. Pull them out of school or move to another district if necessary. Some parents may need to homeschool their kids rather than send them to public schools. It all depends on the student and her inclinations. I strongly support Christian kids who are able to stand strong in public schools. But there may come a time parents need to remove a child from bad influences. Again, this is a weighty decision, one that requires much prayer, wisdom, and counsel.

HANGING OUT WITH REBELLIOUS FRIENDS

Students often surround themselves with others who share the same struggles. If a student is involved in rebellious behavior, he'll gravitate toward like-minded kids. This can mean a whole new set of friends, sometimes forsaking childhood pals who *aren't* rebellious. Usually, obedient students won't hang around those who are rebellious; they don't want to share in the negative and deceptive lifestyle.

This is very apparent when we take students on retreats. The rebellious kids generally sit in the back during meetings, trying to get away from authority figures. We can see it in their posture—arms folded, slouching low, almost defying the speaker to keep their attention. When they see other students standing and worshiping the Lord, the rebellious gang just smirks and sees it as silliness. When the meetings are over, these kids will test the boundaries—big time! If a youth pastor is easily intimidated and wants more than anything else to be their friend, they'll walk all over him. Students in full-blown rebellion don't care what those in authority think of them. They're much more concerned about how they conform with their rebellious friends.

LITTLE SPIRITUAL CONVICTION

Generally, a rebellious student thinks about God very little. Spiritual things only come to mind when parents bring them up, or when forced to be at a church service or youth group. Other than that, rebellious kids have very little fear of God. There's only fear of getting caught. Psalm 36:1 says, "An oracle within my heart concerning the transgression of the wicked: There is no dread of God before his eyes."

When I think of rebellious kids who've gone through our ministry over the years, I'm reminded of Esau in the Bible. If you remember the story, Isaac had two sons, Jacob and Esau. Esau was the firstborn and accordingly deserved much of his father's inheritance. Jacob deceived his father and thus stole the birthright from his brother. When Esau found out, he cried because he lost his inheritance. His tears, however, were not tears of repentance (Heb. 12:16–17). Rather, he was angry at what he'd lost. This is similar to how rebellious children see the world—life is unfair and God is unjust. In fact, this is how many students justify their rebellious behavior.

Along with this comes criticism of those who follow Christ. Rebellious students will point out all the negatives concerning the church. They may complain about students being in cliques, but in reality it's their own attitudes that keep them from having good friends. Parents, don't believe every bad thing your child tells you about the church youth group. A critical heart will speak a distorted message.

SHARP, ANGRY, AND HATEFUL WORDS

It's no surprise that out of a rebellious heart will flow difficult words, for "'what comes out of the mouth comes from the heart'" (Matt. 15:18a). Sometimes a child will say things like, "I hate you." She'll speak this way with her brothers and sisters as well, calling them names and making everyone in the family miserable. In fact, anyone who doesn't feed her self-centered, arrogant world is her enemy, and she'll use hateful words to try to prove that point. I recently talked with a dad who told me of his son's hateful language—swear words full of disrespect and anger. This dad said, "It's hollowing me out. I can barely stand to hear my boy talk this way."

Parents of these kids often feel relieved when the student is not in the house. One young girl caught in rebellion was defiant at every level. Whenever she was home, the tension with her parents was thick; when she was at school, however, the home experienced peace. This is one more obvious sign that rebellion has invaded a household.

A FINAL WORD

Parents with a rebellious child generally don't feel the reward of raising kids as much as they feel the shame. Yet God understands how these parents feel. Israel was rebellious for most of its history, and the Father's heart grew weary with the Israelites' rebellious acts (Mal. 2:17). Remember, no one faces any temptation not common to man, and with it God will provide a way of escape (1 Cor. 10:13). God will help you if you're dealing with a rebellious child.

CHAPTER NINE

Steering Kids Away from Rebellion

A few years ago a girl in our ministry fell in love with a nice guy from her school. He was not a Christian, but he began coming to church and getting involved in the youth ministry. The girl's mother, a single mom, gave her daughter a lot of freedom despite misgivings, primarily because she wanted to maintain a good relationship with the girl.

As the young couple's relationship became more intense, the mother was concerned. She saw that her daughter and this boy were nearly inseparable, and his lack of spiritual convictions concerned her. Before long the mom found out her daughter was lying to her, which undermined their relationship. To make matters worse, the boyfriend began to turn the daughter against her mom.

One afternoon this dear lady came to see me, seeking advice regarding her situation. She made it clear she didn't approve of the relationship, but the daughter was determined to keep it going. This poor mom was worn out by all the conflict and was tempted to just let things go. "After all," she explained, "maybe this boy isn't as bad as I think he is." Above everything else, she didn't want to damage her friendship with her daughter.

I advised her to "go to war" for her daughter. I reminded her she was a mom first and a friend second. This generation needs parents who will go to war for the children, not just leave them to their own desires. Understandably, this mom wasn't sure she wanted to escalate the conflict. I encouraged her to stop being "Mom the friend" and begin setting boundaries. I wanted her to realize that her girl was worth the fight.

I asked the mom, "Do you believe that God wants them to date?" "Absolutely not!" came the reply.

"Are you sure?" I pressed.

"Yes. Emphatically!" she responded.

"If that's true," I reminded her, "then why the questioning? I encourage you to stand strong."

Confronting a rebellious child is an amazing amount of work. This mom knew if she fought her daughter on this issue, it wasn't going to be fun. Still, I saw steel in her eyes as she said, "OK, I'm going to fight for my girl, whether she appreciates it or not." It didn't matter how many mistakes Mom may have made in the past—she was now going to war for her girl.

Students remember these things once they grow out of rebellion. I know people who today have great respect for parents who fought for them during their teen years. I also know kids who lack respect for parents who were too passive. The strong-willed child appreciates strength, even though she won't admit it at the time. This mom was concerned her daughter was going to hate her for taking a stand, but she also knew her daughter would one day be thankful.

Here's what the mom did. She went home that evening and informed her daughter the relationship with this boy was over. Under no circumstances was the girl to see this boy, call him, or continue contact. She made it clear that if it continued, she would enroll her daughter in a different school. "I'll do whatever it takes to remove him from your life," she told her daughter. She'd said similar things in the past, but this time Mom was holding to her boundaries, and the girl knew it.

As you can imagine, this was a difficult time for both of them. The girl became bitter and resentful. Then the boy-friend revealed his true colors by becoming aggressive. One evening in a fit of anger, he tried to break down the front door of their house. He was unsuccessful, but you can imagine the fear this brought to both the mom and daughter. Thankfully, this traumatic incident opened the daughter's eyes to his true character. After that she wanted nothing to do with him.

I'm happy to report that by going to war, the mom saved her daughter from a disastrous path. To this day, the girl is walking strong with Christ. She's now married to a godly man and is doing great. Best of all, she has great respect for her mom and is grateful she did the hard thing. Life might be very different for this girl today if her mom hadn't gone to war.

I don't imply that every situation should be handled this same way. Each unique circumstance requires discernment and wisdom. James 1:5 tells us to seek wisdom from God, and He will give it to us. Proverbs 19:20 says wisdom comes from an abundance of wise counsel. We're also told, "for you should wage war with sound guidance—victory comes with many counselors" (Prov. 24:6). Parents, we can't handle these challenges on our own—we need others in our lives to pray for us and encourage us as we battle for our children. The particular way this mom dealt with her daughter may not work in every situation. The important thing is she went to war for her child, and it paid off.

DADS AND REBELLION

Men, our challenge when dealing with rebellion is to find the balance between two extremes: passivity and anger. Dads, don't be passive. It's crucial that you lead the charge when it comes to raising kids, especially when there's rebellion in the home. Some men are passive because of an attitude that says, "Hey, I was no saint when I was a kid. Sometimes students will paint the town red, but they'll come back again." Kids may or may not come back, but why allow them to make the same mistakes you made? Instead, teach them to do better. These dads need to realize that "painting the town red" is another term for sin. And sin is nothing to take lightly; it has real and lasting consequences.

Other dads are passive by personality. They are naturally aloof, something that hurts kids and frustrates moms terribly. These dads must learn to be involved and proactive in their kids' lives. They need to understand their family is their greatest legacy.

Then there are those of us who don't have a passive bone in our body; the issue is anger. I believe anger is the primary means by which we "exasperate" our children, something we're warned against in Ephesians 6:4a (NIV). This happens when we let our anger overtake us. Some of us feel the only way to deal with rebellious children is to "put them in their place." We explode all over them, then find it only makes things worse. It's true that strong-willed kids respond to strength but not strength out of control. Uncontrolled anger frustrates our kids and will eventually embitter them against us.

But, men, there's a better way. Instead of reacting to students with passivity or uncontrolled anger, be Spirit-controlled. As we're filled with God's Holy Spirit, He promises to give us the self-control needed to deal with rebellion in a godly manner. Only in this way can our anger be contained.

Don't get me wrong—I'm not talking about a passive, milquetoast approach, in which Dad turns into a wimp. Jesus was anything but a wimp; He was the perfect model of real strength, yet He modeled strength under God's control. Remember, just because we're bigger and stronger and can yell louder than our kids, we don't have the right to fly into a rage. Anger feels good for the moment but over time will cost us our family's respect. Proverbs 29:11 says, "A fool gives full vent to his anger, but a wise man holds it in check."

To be honest, I hate rebellion when it shows up in my kids. But I've learned that if I lose control and start yelling, I'll inevitably say things I shouldn't. Men, if you're given to anger and have a difficult time controlling yourself, get help in this area before you deal with a child in rebellion. Find counseling if necessary. Otherwise, your anger may do more harm than good; you might alienate your child during the years he needs you most. If this happens, moms often feel the need to come to the child's rescue, which can lead to major division in the home.

I'm not saying there's no place for anger—rebellion against God and family should make us angry. Ephesians 4:26a says, "Be angry and do not sin." There are times when God gets angry, as He often was with the rebellious children of Israel. But anger must stay under the control of the Holy Spirit. Screaming and physical outbursts are unacceptable for men of God. When we feel ire rising in our bones and are tempted to pick a sassy kid up by his ears, remember God calls us to a higher plane. Christian men are to act like Christ, for all of His resources are at our disposal. If anger is getting the best of you, admit it to a friend, then seek help. Do whatever it takes to keep your anger under control. Otherwise, your home will be full of people walking on eggshells.

Moms and Rebellion

Moms tend to react to rebellion in one of two ways. The first is by pretending it doesn't exist. Children often find it easier to talk to Mom than to Dad, and this is true for the rebellious child as well. Moms are usually more compassionate and generally not so quick to get angry. Students feel they can express themselves to her without getting a huge reaction. Compassion is wonderful, but moms must be careful not to enable rebellion by making excuses for bad behavior. We need to admit rebellion when it surfaces and see it for what it is. Pretending it doesn't exist does only damage—it never solves the problem.

Some moms, however, will respond differently. Rather than being overly compassionate, they decide to take control of the situation. Moms are usually keyed in to their child's feelings and behavior long before dads take notice. If the husband is somewhat aloof or preoccupied with work, a mom can feel very lonely in the battle. The natural feeling is that of panic—"If I don't take charge now, no one will."

An example of this is a conversation I had with a mom some time ago. She told me her teenage boy hated her. When asked why, she complained her husband was too slow to correct the boy's rebellion, so she took it on herself to make sure things were "out in the open." This mom had a strong personality, with a habit of immediately saying everything that came to mind. She was quick to point out problems—

basically, quick to nag. Her young man needed Dad's presence, mentoring, and leadership, but though the husband was doing his best, it wasn't fast enough for Mom. She was stealing the position of authority from her husband, and it embittered the son toward her.

Being strong willed is not bad, but ladies must make sure their will is placed under the control of God's Spirit. Like any trait, it can overflow its boundaries and create havoc and harm.

Without trying to step on toes, I need to say that women with overly strong personalities can sometimes create passive sons. A sensitive boy will have difficulty standing up to Mom; he may find it easier to clam up rather than risk sharing his thoughts. Later in life, this can result in a man who lacks confidence or has difficulty making decisions. On the other hand, an overly strong mom with a strong-willed boy can result in an explosive mix.

However, many dads refuse to take leadership. What can a wife do if her husband refuses to deal with rebellion? First, Mom, slow down, take a deep breath, and be careful to maintain self-control in your response. Let the kids see that you respect your husband and his God-given authority. Second, look for opportunities to let your husband lead, even in small things. He may actually want to take leadership yet feels stifled by your quicker verbal skills. It may be that he's slower to respond than you would like, or might even disagree with you on how some things should be handled. I'm not saying he's always right. But give him the benefit of the doubt. Work with your husband, not against him. Be his greatest supporter, not one who readily undermines his authority. Just as men need to submit their anger to God, you need to submit your strength of will to the Holy Spirit. Do all you can to work together as a team, even if it means lowering some of your own expectations. Otherwise, a child in rebellion may actually tear your marriage apart—an unspeakable tragedy that doesn't need to happen.

THE HEART OF THE PARENT

When it comes to rebellion, I'm reminded of the story of the Prodigal Son in Luke 15. Notice that the dad wasn't rebuked as a poor father. Instead, this was a wise and loving man who treated his sons well. He didn't deserve the pain he endured because of his son's poor choices.

I know parents who have done a great job and yet have a wayward child. They've done Bible studies with their kids, gone on family outings, and poured their lives into their children. Other parents have done a so-so job, and yet their kids have turned out great. I don't understand why this happens, but it does. I do know, however, that God is in control.

For instance, I know of one family that seemed to do everything right; the parents homeschooled their kids and raised them in a godly manner. They even had their kids sit in adult classes to hear the Scriptures. It never crossed their minds that one day rebellion might enter their household.

Unfortunately, when their oldest girl graduated from high school, she immediately fell in love with a guy and became pregnant. The second daughter did the same, also walking away from the Lord. These dear parents became very disillusioned, to the point that it negatively impacted their own walk with Christ. As Christians, they were not only concerned with their daughters' welfare but with their own reputation. It's been a very difficult road for these parents to travel.

Within the Christian subculture, rebellious children are rarely tolerated. Instead, we immediately cast stones at parents, forgetting that even good parents can experience rebellious kids. Sometimes it's the parents of younger children who are most critical of others. Their own kids aren't old enough to rebel, which means they've not yet experienced what it's like to raise teenagers. Younger couples may find themselves saying, "I thought there was something not right about their parenting. They're way too strict," or "They're way too lenient." It's easy to be critical of others.

When my own kids have played with rebellion, I have to be honest—my concern isn't only for them but also for my image as a parent. We all want others to think well of us, and we cringe when we're accused of poor parenting. When Sue and I had our first two kids, they usually did well in public. At the grocery store I would see other children screaming, crawling out of the cart, and being obnoxious. I would think to myself, "If those people were good parents, they'd have their kids under control." Then came my youngest child, who made all other kids look like Mother Teresa. Now when I see a parent struggling with an out-of-control kid, I want to walk up and say, "Hey, we should start a support group. Hang in there. I know exactly how you feel."

I encourage you to come alongside families struggling with wayward kids. How can you do this? First, don't come across like the counselors of Job, who told him everything they thought he was doing wrong. Instead, be there and show support. Second, speak little and listen much. Spend time praying with and for these parents and ask God to return the prodigal child to the family. Third, don't allow yourself to believe that if you were the parent, you would automatically have things under control. Think of rebellious Esau. Could you have raised him better than Isaac did? You don't know all the circumstances involved, and you can't control the will of another.

Fortunately, prodigals usually come back to the faith they've spurned. I think of Jake, a young man in our student ministry. His parents are strong believers and did a great job of raising him in the Lord, but he decided he wanted a taste of the world. He was very open about his wanderings; he went to parties, experimented with drugs and alcohol, and spurned his previous interest in spiritual matters.

Jake's parents were heartbroken, yet they responded to him with grace and firmness. They went to war for him. They let him know he brought them great pain, even though he said he didn't care. They gave him consequences, even though that appeared to have no effect. They insisted he stay involved in the student ministry, though he would sit in the back with his arms folded. They also sought wise counsel and worked with the church's youth leaders, who did their best to pursue Jake.

Eventually, Jake had his fill of waywardness. God restored his soul, and now he's on fire for Christ. He recently stood in front of the youth group and apologized for the disgrace he brought his family and his God; he did this on his own initiative. He's now actively sharing the gospel with his friends, and is doing great with the Lord. He's leading a Bible study with junior high kids and having a positive impact on their lives.

The challenge to all of us is to respond to parents of rebellious children with grace and love. We must be careful how we talk about these hurting families, especially with others. Through the years I've seen many families experience this kind of pain. Personally, I commend many of these parents for keeping the vision for a rebellious son or daughter, even as others criticized their parenting. These are my true heroes. Like the Prodigal Son's dad, they reflect our heavenly Father, who never gives up on us. We should love these families, pray for them, and encourage them as best we can. In this way, we deny the impulse to criticize and teach our children to do the same.

CHAPTER TEN

Let the Church Help You Raise Your Kids

If any one chapter in this book is more important than the others, I believe this is it. Why? It deals with the church, the body of Christ. A parent may wonder, "What does going to church have to do with parenting this emerging generation?" It's a good question and one we'll address over the next few pages.

Many are surprised when I tell them this generation of students has a hunger for the church. Today's students are often more hungry for church than their parents are. This is a generation that loves community. Our kids understand this concept because the world has defined itself in such terms, i.e., the gay community, the arts community, etc. Students desire to be involved in something bigger than themselves. Thus, it should be no surprise that Christian kids will search for this sense of belonging within the local church. God created us for community—never for isolation—and this generation has taken that to heart.

Should Your Kids Go to Church?

I firmly believe that every student who is a believer in Christ needs to be in church on a regular basis (Heb. 10:25). There's no way around it. The world gets a student's attention for many hours each week. A typical teenager is bombarded with worldly messages from TV, radio, and movies. Even if we do our best to protect our kids from harm, we can never escape the fact that we live in a fallen world full of fallen messages. If our kids are to counteract those messages, they must be plugged in to a local church. If not, they're missing the teaching of the Word and the community of believers. Both are crucial for a healthy spiritual life.

I've heard parents say, "I'm not going to push my teenagers to go to church. My parents pushed me, and I didn't like it." My reply? Sometimes we all need to be pushed to do the right thing. Being part of the local church is more than a good idea—it's God's plan for every believer, teenagers included.

Every one of my kids has decided, at one time or another, he or she didn't want to go to church. I have to admit there were times it would have been easier to leave the kids at home. Have you experienced Sunday morning arguments on the way to worship? Hey, that's life with children. Yet no matter how inconvenient, I'm adamant that my kids be at church. It's important they learn to love the body of Christ.

My son Daniel, when in junior high, decided he wasn't going to go to youth group anymore. That made me feel great, being the pastor in charge of the youth ministry. I wanted him to say to me, "Dad, you're so awesome. I hang on your every word when you teach. How wonderful you are." But, no. Those weren't the words coming out of his mouth.

I replied, "OK, Daniel, tell me why you don't want to go."

"Well, the games are dumb, the small groups are boring, and the leaders think they're funny, but they're not," was the answer. "Besides, there are too many nerds, and none of my friends go."

I thought for a minute about what I should say. Something wise—profound. Something that might help him understand the importance of church in God's grand scheme of things. But nothing came to mind, so I just said, "That's nice, son. OK, get in the car or we're going to be late for junior high group." He gave me a look as if to say, "Well, at least I tried," then he jumped in the car and off we went. He needed to be there, whether he felt like it or not.

HOW'S YOUR ATTITUDE?

Parents, do *you* always feel like going to church? If you're honest, you'll admit there are days you'd rather stay in bed. I have days like that, too, and I'm a pastor! It's no wonder, then, that a typical teenager is not going to be thrilled about an early morning church service, especially if he's stayed up late the night before. My response (in their own jargon): "*Whatever!*" When we listen to a kid's excuses (and I'm amazed how many parents do), we not only harm his walk with Christ, but we actually teach him a wrong theology of the church.

Let me explain. If your student tells you, "I don't like the youth group. It's just not my style," and you listen to those excuses and accept them, you've just taught him that going to church is all about him and his tastes. You've taught him to attend church only if he's entertained, it fits his personality, or he hits it off with the youth pastor. He's learned that staying home is an acceptable option.

If we ask parents to evaluate a church service, they'll often do so based on the quality of the message and the power of the worship. If the message wasn't engaging or didn't feed them at a sufficient level, they'll often give it a low grade. "I give the service today a D," they may say on the way home. Is it any wonder, then, that students do the same with the youth group? If we train our kids to have a critical spirit regarding the body of Christ, we shouldn't be surprised if they leave church when they get older. Why would they want to be involved with an institution that never meets their standards?

When the New Testament teaches us about church, it doesn't teach us to grade a worship service based on the quality of performance. Instead, the church is to examine itself in regard to pure teaching. In the book of Revelation, chapters 2 and 3, Jesus Himself examined the churches of the ancient world. But He didn't assess them on their entertainment value. No, Christ was, and is, interested in pure teaching, perseverance in the midst of suffering, and faithfulness to Him in the midst of trials. He said nothing about popularity, entertaining messages, and the quality of the worship band.

Think of the church at Corinth. Many of us would have said to ourselves, "I'm giving up on this church body." It was full of immorality, confusion about spiritual gifts, and division because of personality worship (1 Cor. 1:12). But Paul didn't call people to disband or to leave because of difficulties. No, he encouraged them to stay together and to clean up their act.

I'm not against powerful worship services and well-prepared messages. These things are crucial. I am against teaching our kids we can minimize the role of church in our lives if it doesn't meet our needs. This is a wrong view of church— it's wrong for our students, and it's wrong for us as parents.

The church, the precious bride of Christ, is not about our taste. In fact, it's not really about us at all. We often treat church as one more entertainment experience. "If I like the pastor and he's funny, then I'll go. If he starts preaching on money, then I won't." Notice that Hebrews 10:25 gives a clear command: "not staying away from our meetings, as some habitually do, but encouraging each other, and all the more as you see the day drawing near." It says nothing about meeting together only if it agrees with our personal tastes.

So, what are you teaching your kids about the church? What kind of attitude do you convey when you mention your church's leaders? At His coming, Christ will present the church, His bride, to Himself without spot or wrinkle (Eph. 5:27). Does your attitude help or hinder this process? We can model a good attitude for our children by how we talk about the pastors, the elders, the weekly message, or the youth leaders. The apostle Paul told Titus to stay clear of divisive people (Titus 3:10). Let's be careful that we're not harming the unity of Christ's body. If we are, we're teaching our kids to do the same as they grow up.

If you as a family become militant and angry toward the church and its leaders, it's likely your children will be doubly angry as they grow up. Our children have a way of taking up our causes; if we're not careful, we'll set them up to hate Christ's body. Gossip is a sin—let's be careful not to gossip with our children when we see things we don't like.

So, why should we insist our children attend church? Because church is important for students in the same way it's important for adults. A healthy church never pushes kids away from Christ but instead draws them closer to Him. Any time the Word of God is being taught or read, it will not return empty (Isa. 55:10–11). This holds true, despite the bored look a teenager may have on his face during a worship service. In 2 Timothy 3:16b we're told the Bible is beneficial "for teaching, for rebuking, for correcting, for training in righteousness." God isn't a liar. If your student is exposed to the Word of God on a regular basis, I believe God will do a work in his heart, even though it may not be readily apparent.

Over and over I've seen students whose lives have been transformed by just one message, one speaker, one event. Of course, in reality it's an accumulation of God's work over time. But one message or event can bring it all together. This often happens with students who are forced to attend by their parents. You never know which message may catch your student's attention. For that reason alone, your kids need to be in church on a regular basis.

How to Get Rid of Your Youth Pastor

Let's apply these things to your daughter's youth group. If she struggles with the youth pastor, how you deal with her concerns affords a great opportunity to mentor her in how to love Christ's body.

Most youth pastors only last a year and a half in student ministry. That's the national average. Many factors contribute to this, such as inadequate training or lack of the right gifting. But more often than not, a young man is run out of youth ministry by negative parents who convey negative attitudes. Sometimes a parent will side with his child against a youth pastor, for whatever reason, and then infect other parents with a critical spirit. Before long the youth pastor is out of a job. These parents have just taught their students the wrong way to deal with church conflict.

Recently, a good friend of mine experienced this first-hand. After twenty years of strong youth ministry in a local church, he became the target of a disgruntled elder. The concerns didn't involve sin but rather issues of personal taste. The elder's son didn't enjoy the group, and the father began speaking negatively to other elders regarding the pastor. Soon my friend found himself under a microscope, and before long he was forced to resign. Since then, numbers of people have left the church, including many families with students. It was a tragic situation and totally unnecessary.

The elder should have addressed my friend in a straightforward manner. Instead, he and his wife chose to spread their views by way of gossip and slander. What they did was sin. They took a good man out of an effective ministry.

Sometimes, of course, there are legitimate concerns regarding a youth leader. When that's the case, go to him directly and share your heart. Don't let him hear your concerns from someone else. Offer to do everything you can to help him, preserve him, and work with him. Of course, there are instances where a man is not fit for ministry, such as when sin is involved. Sin must be dealt with immediately with firmness. Yet statistics show that many youth pastors are forced out of churches for the wrong reasons. If your concerns fall in the category of personal taste or philosophical differences, be careful not to stir things up unnecessarily. Always seek to build up Christ's body, rather than tear it down.

THE PROPER APPROACH

As a youth pastor, I have no problem with parents who share their concerns with me. It happens all the time. I welcome good input, especially when given in an attitude of support and encouragement. What isn't helpful, though, is when parents go around me by talking directly with the senior pastor. One family in our church became upset but decided not to confront me directly. Instead, the family went to the lead pastor and began sharing concerns. When our lead pastor heard the nature of the complaints, he immediately said, "Well, let's bring in Steve and discuss it together." What a great response. I could tell by the parents' faces as I entered the room they weren't thrilled at my invitation to the meeting. Still, it was the right thing to do. They should have come to me in the first place.

I am shocked at how some parents talk about the church to their students. I know from experience, as well as from colleagues around the country, that many parents are openly disrespectful to those in ministry. If parents can talk harshly to a pastor, often in public, it makes me wonder what kinds of things are said in the privacy of their homes. I'm not implying that pastors are above criticism, not at all. Pastors should be above reproach in their lifestyle and conduct, but no pastor is flawless. Paul exhorted Titus to be blameless, but that in no way implies perfection (Titus 1:6–7). Some parents need to remove the log from their own eyes before being critical of others (Matt. 7:5). It's often the attitude behind the criticism, however, that so easily contaminates our children.

I feel honored when parents come to me and say, "Steve, I need some help with my kid. What do I do?" or "Steve, I appreciate what you're doing for my son, but he's not connecting with the ministry." I'll help any way I can. But when parents come at me with a critical spirit, it's often deflating and counterproductive. In fact, the worst thing a parent can say to me is, "I've talked with other families and we all feel the same way." Please don't do that to your youth pastor. If you have concerns, go to him directly. After all, we're all on the same side.

HOW TO ENCOURAGE YOUR YOUTH PASTOR

So what kinds of things can parents do to encourage and support the youth pastor? First, be aware there are many legitimate ways of doing student ministry. Your church's youth pastor has a distinct personality, and he'll run the ministry according to his personal tastes and gifting. That doesn't mean he can't change—merely that he's wired to do ministry a certain way. If you're uncomfortable with his style of ministry, think long and hard before you make it a divisive issue, especially in front of your kids.

Second, understand there is no such thing as a perfect youth ministry. Sure, there are some basic components that need to exist, such as solid Bible teaching. But teaching can, and will, take many forms. One leader may be inclined toward theological issues, another toward introducing seekers to Christ. Or maybe a leader isn't great from the pulpit, but he shines when leading small-group Bible studies. Allow for flexibility—don't demand that he be the best communicator in the world. If he needs help, then find him good training. Pay for it if you need to. Don't merely write him off because he's not meeting your high expectations. Work with him—find ways to help him develop. Along with these things, maybe the best thing you can do is give him time to mature.

Years ago some of our students had a hard time paying attention when a certain leader taught in our ministry. "Steve, is so-and-so teaching tonight?" they'd say to me. "If he is, we don't want to go. He's too boring."

I told them, "Guys, this man loves Christ, and he's got some good things to say. You need to go and listen anyway." I stood by this leader because of the potential I saw in him. You know what? These boys continued to attend, and before long this leader was discipling them all, having a powerful influence in their lives. I'm so glad I didn't say, "Yeah, you're right. He's not the best teacher in the world. In fact, he's not nearly as good as he thinks he is, so you can wait for the exceptional teachers." Imagine what these young men, and their families, would have lost. Be wise in helping your students love the church, even when it's not extremely entertaining.

Third, remember that games and activities are normal, even crucial, when ministering to students. Games are not inherently unspiritual. Some parents complain about games during youth group evenings. I feel like saying, "Well, your adult Sunday school spends twenty-five minutes eating before you get into your study. Which is healthier—shooting basketball or eating doughnuts?" Of course, I'd never say that, but we all have our different forms of entertainment. There's nothing wrong with enjoying time together over coffee and pastries, just as there's nothing wrong in playing basketball before Bible study. Let's not pretend our chosen forms of entertainment don't exist.

Fourth, remember that if students go on retreats and weekend outings and come back on a spiritual high, that's OK. I know it's going to wear off after a few days, but there's nothing wrong with getting excited about Jesus and letting it color their world for awhile. I love it when students get reenergized about the Lord. I don't want them to live for their emotions, but I realize that emotions are a part of life. I don't criticize them because they're emotional beings.

Some parents will say, "Well, that's just emotionalism." Not if God's working. God uses emotions to help us stay engaged. Imagine if you were teaching a Bible study and no one cracked a smile or showed any kind of response whatsoever. You'd wonder if your teaching was having any impact at all. You'd probably want to quit. My point is this: There's nothing wrong with falling in love with Jesus and letting our emotions reveal that.

By the way, when your kids go on a retreat, pray diligently for safety and wisdom for those in leadership. We live in a litigation culture, and it's very risky these days for a youth pastor to take kids away for a weekend. Several years ago as our students headed home from a retreat, one of our vans—full of students—flipped on the freeway. I was driving ahead of the accident, and as I raced back to the scene, I was sure I'd find students dead and dying. Thankfully, the worst injury required only six stitches to a young girl's knee. We were amazed at God's hand of protection and shuddered at what might have happened. Later, we found out a mom had woken up the night before and felt prompted to pray diligently for the safety of our kids. She was somehow convinced there was going to be an accident, and she prayed that no one would be hurt. How grateful we were for answered prayer!

Of course, during accidents like this comes the inevitable scrutiny. Parents need to be able to trust those in leadership and hold leaders accountable for their actions. In this case there was wonderful maturity on the part of the parents involved. They could have easily crucified our student ministry team, but they didn't; they chose to believe the best about us as leaders. I was grateful for such grace on the part of these parents. Hard questions were asked, but the prevailing attitude was that of support and encouragement. Christ was honored by the way things were handled.

VOLUNTEERING—THE ANTIDOTE TO CRITICISM

A number of years ago a few parents got together and decided our ministry to students wasn't deep enough theologically. (Others had said, of course, that it was *too* deep.) They became quite vocal about their concerns. I carefully listened to them and then encouraged them to get involved as volunteers. Before long they fell in love with the ministry. In fact, they became very supportive of what we were doing. From a distance they had been critical, but once they got up close and took personal ownership, their attitudes began to change. Those who are most involved are usually the ones who criticize the least.

It used to be said that students don't want their parents involved at youth group. This generation, though, doesn't mind nearly as much. Most students will say it's no big deal if their parents attend. I encourage moms and dads to volunteer with student ministries, but to do so for the sake of ministry; I don't want them there to spy on their kids. If parents come to help, I need them to work with the ministry and not against it. I know our youth ministry isn't perfect, mainly because I'm not perfect. I also know I can't please everyone.

Youth pastors are generally thankful when parents get involved. It's great when parents show up to help with activities, serve food, and help lead Bible studies. In our ministry we have a "star team" made up of parents that regularly attend our events. They know what's happening in the ministry and are able to talk with other parents who may have concerns.

Finally, the best way to support a youth pastor is by encouraging his vision. He's doing a difficult job because he wants to have an impact on students for Christ. The great majority of youth leaders are in ministry for the right reasons, and we need to thank them for their efforts. By coming alongside the youth pastor and encouraging his ministry, you'll be teaching your students the proper way to both support the church and respond to authority (1 Pet. 5:5).

Epilogue

In the introduction to this book I talked about an annual banquet for our graduating seniors. Every year I challenge our students to make sure they grow and mature in the Lord. I tell them, "These have been good years, but don't allow them to be the best years of your life."

If you've been to a twenty-year reunion, you've seen classmates who haven't changed a bit since high school—it's almost as if their personalities are frozen in time. When I went to my reunion, I was looking forward to seeing people I hadn't seen in years. Of course, when I arrived, I found most of us had a few more pounds and a lot less hair than we used to. All of us had changed physically, but amazingly some people had changed little emotionally. One guy, who used to be a good buddy, was now trapped in alcoholism and a hedonistic lifestyle. Though he was thirty-eight years old, talking to him was like conversing with a very immature high school student. There are high schoolers in our ministry who are more mature in both wisdom and choices than this man. It was sad, and it reminded me that Satan wants to keep us trapped in emotional and spiritual immaturity.

As parents and mentors to this next generation, it's our responsibility, along with the body of Christ, to encourage our sons and daughter to never get stuck spiritually and emotionally. That's why I use the banquet to get students thinking about what they will be like in ten or fifteen years. I challenge them to look at their high school and college years as good days but to not let them be their best days.

Here, then, are five ways I encourage them to keep that from happening:

1. I challenge students to continue to fix their eyes on Christ, the Source and Perfecter of our faith (Heb. 12:2), for He will cause them to grow up in Christ.

2. I challenge them to protect their names, for "a good name is to be chosen over great wealth" (Prov. 22:1a). As they grow, they will mature in Christ, so that their names bring honor to God, as well as to their families.

3. I challenge students to pursue great friends. My daughter Kristy was recently married, and all of the bridesmaids and groomsmen were great friends she and her husband had developed over the years. Every one of them has a zealous walk with Christ, and they've helped each other remain consistent in their faith. Without godly friends, our students will have little chance of staying the course.

4. I challenge students to honor their parents. It's not until they have kids of their own that they'll fully realize how much love parents have for their children. I think of this every time a student gets hurt in a horrible accident. The first day at the hospital is when dozens of fellow students show up to support the friend. After two weeks, it's only the student's best friends. After two months, it's only the family.

Scripture is clear that we are to honor our fathers and our mothers (Eph. 6:2).

5. I challenge students to be in church every week—no excuses. It's wrong theology to believe that a person can grow in Christ apart from the church. The Bible is clear when it says we are not to be "staying away from our meetings, as some habitually do" (Heb. 10:25a).

Moms and dads, someday your kids will be gone, and the house will be emptier than you can imagine. I believe you must teach the above qualities, and others listed in this book, to your kids if they're to live zealously for Christ. Whatever the effort on your part, it will be worth it. There can be no greater reward than to see your children fulfill God's purpose for their lives, both now and in the future.

Let's be zealous to mentor this next generation in the love and obedience of Christ.

If you have any questions or comments
you'd like to talk with Steve about, feel free to e-mail him:
steve.keels@goodshepherdcc.org.